CATASTROPHIC RIGHTS

Catastrophic
Rights

Experimental Drugs & AIDS

John Dixon

New Star Books   *Vancouver · 1990*

First printing March 1990.
1 2 3 4 5   94 93 92 91 90

Canadian Cataloguing in Publication Data

Dixon, John Edward, 1943-
  Catastrophic rights

ISBN 0-921586-08-6 (bound). - ISBN 0-921586-07-8 (pbk.)
1. AIDS (Disease) – Chemotherapy.   2. Drugs – Testing – Government policy.   3. Terminally ill – Civil rights   4. Sick – Legal status, laws, etc.
1. Title.
RC607.A26D59 1990   362.1'969792   C90-091092-5

The publisher is grateful for assistance provided by the Canada Council and the Cultural Services Branch, Province of British Columbia.

New Star Books Ltd.
2504 York Avenue
Vancouver, B.C.
CANADA V6K 1E3

Printed and bound in Canada.

Contents

Preface

THIS IS an essay about a single aspect of one of the great crises of our time. The crisis is the AIDS epidemic, and my special concern is with patients' access to unproven drugs.

In one sense, the essay will be out of date by the time it is printed. New AIDS drugs (such as Bristol-Myers' DDI) will be in fairly common use soon, and others (hopefully even more effective and less toxic) will enter the strife-torn path from laboratory to clinic. In order to stay abreast of these hoped-for developments, this book would have to be revised on a biannual basis.

I am, however, much more concerned with the path than with the individual travellers. The issue of access to catastrophic therapies will be confronted over and over again at each step on the way to the goal shared by medical science, patients, and society – the complete conquest of HIV infection. So this is not a book about treatments as such, but about the moral and political responsibility of medicine and government to attend to the special claims of their erstwhile partners – the catastrophically ill – in the quest for treatments.

I bring neither radical sensibilities nor a radical agenda to my task. I am, rather, a moderate civil libertarian who has an affectionate respect for the efforts of democratic states to govern in the public interest, and a bemused tolerance for the strengths and weaknesses of the free enterprise system.

I have no villains to offer up in a flourish of investigative virtuosity. But something terrible *is* happening. Justice is not being done to the significance of the distinction between ordinary and catastrophic illness. And even when the distinction itself is made – as is more often the case recently – its significance for the operation of our therapeutic systems is not being thought through and translated into appropriate reforms. The result is that dying people continue to be denied their legitimate right to a greater than ordinary say in how they fight for their own lives.

My purpose here is to make a first effort at mapping out the terrain of catastrophic rights. More can be done, more should be done, and more will be done. But a start must be made immediately, and the work in hand is my response to the immediate need. It was constructed on the base of a paper which I presented at the Fifth International AIDS Conference in June 1989 at Montreal. As I acknowledged at the time, Kevin Brown, of the Vancouver Persons With AIDS Society, was the source of indispensable advice and encouragement in that first effort. Mr. Brown gave the principal address at the opening plenary session of the Montreal Conference by videotape, since he died a few weeks before the conference.

Several philosophers with the British Columbia Civil Liberties Association – Dr. Alister Browne, Dale Beyerstein and Dr. John Westwood, made important contributions to this book. John Russell – past Executive Director of the BCCLA and now at Cornell University – made particularly insightful critical comments, as did Professor Robert Rowan of the University of California at San Diego, and Professor Emeritus Joseph Tussman of the University of California at Berkeley. Professor Philip Bryden of the University of British Columbia Law Faculty was a steadying rock of common sense, urging the forms of practical modesty which cannot be overvalued when the object of the exercise is to produce a useful direction for policy.

I am particularly indebted, for their medical advice, to Dr. Michael Weaver, clinical immunologist at St. Paul's Hospital in Vancouver, Prof. Martin Schechter, head of AIDS research at the Faculty of Medicine of the University of B.C., and Dr. Andrew Wilkinson – a Director of the BCCLA who enjoys the advantage of being a practising lawyer as well as a physician. Dr. Michelle Brill-Edwards, the Assistant Medical Director of the Canadian Federal Health Protection Branch, provided invaluable factual advice in connection with the work of her department.

Finally, however, two men – Greig Layne of the Vancouver Persons With Aids Society, and philosopher/writer/civil libertarian Stan Persky – were most responsible for my undertaking this work and carrying it through. Beside his instigating and sustaining energy, it was one of Persky's many good ideas to call these special patients' rights "catastrophic." Greig Layne supplied inexhaustible stores of inspiration at the outset in Montreal, and wielded a sharp editorial pen as the project neared completion.

My editor at New Star, Audrey McClellan, has indefatigably fished for errors and infelicities in the roiling depths of the manuscript. The mistakes that readers find were almost certainly hooked by Audrey first, only to be stubbornly restored to the waters by me. I owe a great debt to Russell Wodell of the BCCLA staff, who provided me, in his remarkable and singular self, with a researcher, editorial assistant, congenial colleague, plus the fastest keyboard in the country.

Readers should be more than routinely alert to the fact that I bear sole responsibility for all of the errors of fact and judgment in this book. None of those who have been kind enough to help me – either openly or in confidence – should be accused of subscribing to any of my arguments, or the positions which rest upon them. To the extent, however, that any portion of truth or justice is uncovered by any part of this work, then that is the part that properly belongs to the memory of Kevin Brown and the inspiration of Greig Layne.

I.
Introduction

IN THE mid-Seventies, the press became fascinated with the menace of Killer Bees. They were a fierce African strain of honey-bees that had been inadvertently or foolishly introduced to South America, had escaped the domestic control of their keepers, and were heading North. The news story played out over a period of years like a diffuse War of the Worlds broadcast ("Can they be held at the Canal!?"), and the Killer Bees became yet another element of the anxious background noise of modernity.

They were perfect for their media role. To start with, they had the prime-time characteristics of absolutely mindless ferocity and barbarian "otherness." We knew that if they ever got a chance, they would fall on us with a buzzing, tropical craziness, and that our tender bodies would simply be undone by their atavistic ravishings. But best of all, contrary to all predictions and warnings, and indispensably for their surreal function, they never turned up.

There is, in 1990, for many North Americans and Europeans, a profound connection between the Killer Bee and AIDS stories. Because although it is obvious that AIDS eventually came, and came in force, it is also obvious that it was so far from even-handed in the distribution of its horrors that, for First World heterosexuals at least, it has not yet fulfilled its terrible promise as a killer. What is more, and just as in the Killer Bee legend,

AIDS came (monkeys to Africans to . . .) in the classical horror story guise of the exotic, foreign, Other; in broad epidemiological terms, it concentrated its attack upon a group among us who were already marked off as apart, mysterious, sexually other.

There are even jokes about the non-existent heterosexual AIDS epidemic, but they are delivered a bit shame-facedly and *sotto voce* by most who tell them, not only because they are dirtied by the terrible suffering of others, but because everybody knows that the last laugh about AIDS may well be one that they have no taste (or breath) to join in.

Now a different metaphor looms: the story of the Sitzkrieg or Phoney War of the opening months of the Second World War. The Enemy stalled after the first breathtaking display of his power and ruthlessness (only Poland! only Gays! Maybe we can deal with this . . .), and hope rises that the general alarm was a false one. The fear that now haunts us is that AIDS is, as the Nazis were, only at a pause, that it is still coming for us all – first, as always, for our young in the front line of the physically active – that it is really just a matter of time. The continuing fuss about condom-dispensers over at the high-school (how should the ads go? "a stitch in time," "you've come a long way baby," or "emergency only! heavy penalties provided by law") burns the point in. If we're still carrying our gas-masks around, the war isn't over. The next big strategic move of the enemy depends (in this nightmare) upon how long the kindling base of infection in the homosexual, bisexual, and drug addict populations takes to break out into a general and perhaps unquenchable conflagration.

Of course, everyone's imagination is as different as their experiences and wants, and in North America there is a huge gulf between the heterosexual images of AIDS and the gay ones. Gays aren't thinking about AIDS in terms of Killer Bees and the Sitzkrieg. In centres such as San Francisco, New York, L.A., and my home of Vancouver, the sense is of holocaust, of cosmic injustice, and of dread that is not dulled by exhaustion and repletion, but made ever more keen. The *Names* quilt project, which seeks at once to humanize the carnage and bring it to the senses of all of us (thus hopefully bringing us to our senses about what is really happening), confronts us with an overwhelming, simply stupefying experience of scale. And after scale, youth. We are not accustomed to thinking, outside the context of a big shooting war, of so many young people killed all at once.

The gay community, never as natural a grouping as those outside believe it to be, has been subtly divided by the emergency. Is it to be "into the streets," demanding adequate treatment for its casualties? Or into some form of public relations closet in the hope of avoiding the homophobia that reins in some of the political sources of help? (Although in this connection, I suspect that we need an additional word that connotes not so much *fear* of homosexuals, but rather a profound, heterosexually-biased *indifference* to them and their world. Not all "us/them" dichotomies are born of fear.)

And finally, just to round out the store of images, there is the business of who we are to bring to mind as having or likely to have this disease . . . the familiar triad of gays, intravenous drug abusers, and hemophiliacs. For each in their own way (if I may continue to speak in broad – and hence important – generalities) it is a nightmare of misidentification and guilt by association. The gays scream: "We're not drug addicts!" The drug addicts straighten up to yell: "We're not faggots!" And the hemophiliacs (who, along with those born infected, are often called the "innocent victims") are so upset with their brothers and sisters-in-suffering that, given an either/or choice, they would prefer not be thought of at all rather than thought of in their company. AIDS has tended to make not just strange bedfellows, but mutually repulsed bedfellows.

So AIDS is a story that everybody is tired of – albeit for very different reasons – but which refuses to go away. It smolders along, spinning off brush fires of journalistic enthusiasm from time to time, but continues to draw mainstream media coverage not so much for what it has done, or does, as for what it could very well yet do.

This is a small book about a small part of the story – the struggle of AIDS patients for the right to a bigger say in how they are medically treated. Initially, I got involved in it for a couple of reasons, one of them institutional, and the other personal. First of all, I am the president of the B.C. Civil Liberties Association, which is the oldest rights body in Canada, with a long working experience of discrimination and patients' rights issues. And secondly, one of my dearest friends – a gay writer – was absolutely sure that he had AIDS, and I sweated out the period of waiting for the test results with him – negative. But finally, I became really absorbed by the issue because of the men in the Persons With Aids Society of Vancouver, whose requests for help were so civilized and courageously modulated as to be irresistible.

I was, to be honest, terrified of them at first. Of course, I was as well versed as anyone about the very limited infectiousness of their disease, but it is such a terrible, dooming disease, that I was really afraid of its very nearness in them. I can recall that on my first visit to their office, over in the gay part of town, they answered their phone and said that it was for me – some sort of message from my secretary. I took the telephone receiver in my hand, and was instantly reminded of the Lenny Bruce bit in which the Southern Liberal is offered a lighted cigarette by a Black, and says: "Ah . . . sure . . . I can put that out for you." All of that passed, of course, but I still believe that there is very little mileage to be had in making fun of people who are afraid of catching an infectious, incurable, stigmatizing, and terminal disease – whether they're telephone installers or surgeons.

But before I begin to talk about PWAs and their rights to experimental drugs, it is necessary to back up a bit and consider exactly what it is that they have, and how we have dealt with it. I offer this account diffidently, not because I'm not a physician, but because the most judicious physicians continue to offer the medical facts about AIDS diffidently. There is a lot about it that we do not yet know, and it is at least possible that some of what we think we know will be proven false. Clinicians have called syphilis – that other terrible STD, with literally millions of deaths to its historical credit – "the great impostor" because of its ability to mimic so many other diseases. AIDS seems to have inherited some of this familial power with its protean ability to elude having its medical facts nailed down. In any case, I offer what we know with the caveat that the book is very far from closed on the medical story.

I rush to add that does not mean that the modes of transmission of the disease are in doubt. These are facts which depend for their verification, not so much upon the accuracy of our medical account, as on the clinical and epidemiological evidence – and that is in.

The first thing to attend to is the fundamental importance of the fact that the AIDS "germ" is a virus rather than a bacterium. (A retro-virus actually, a side issue not essential to the main outline of the picture.) The difference between these two sources of infection is that, generally speaking, bacteria are self-sufficient organisms that exist outside the cells of our body, while viruses are incomplete organisms that can only live by incorporating themselves within other living cells. They manage this by taking over part of the target cell's machinery for maintaining its own life. That makes it, naturally and generally, much easier to kill – pick off – bacteria without damaging the cells of the patient than is the case with viruses. Hence, we have a very broad range of enormously effective antibiotics that work nothing short of wonders with the diseases that are caused by bacterial infection such as, say, syphilis, but we have very little with which to directly attack the viral causes of the common cold.

So viruses are bad news for which we have, as yet, only very weak medical responses. They are a direct source of much of the sort of trouble that we experience as illness, and – perhaps worse yet – an indirect cause or trigger of a really huge proportion of human sickness. This is because cells or tissue that have been killed or damaged by a viral infection form a trouble spot that is peculiarly susceptible to the most persistent forms of bacterial infection, or, as in the case of a range of cancers, virally damaged cells can lose control of their normal ability to limit their growth, and quite literally go on a crazed and ultimately self-destructive expansive binge.

As if this isn't bad enough, the AIDS virus is a special sort of viral disaster in that its target is the system of specialized cells that recognize infections of invasive organisms and fight them off. Thus, death from the Acquired Immune Deficiency Syndrome is always indirect in that AIDS opens the door – and keeps it open – for other infections that we would normally handle with ease. It is a fifth column capable of rendering us absolutely defenseless against any of our infectious enemies by destroying the immune system's capacity for either recognizing non-self invaders or doing anything about them. This explains the truly exotic range of illnesses that characterize the "opportunistic infections" of AIDS, such as Kaposi's sarcoma and pneumocystis; diseases that an ordinary general practitioner could expect to see once or never in a life-time of North American medical experience.

All diseases that aspire to being more than a transitory blip in the experience of a single host cell or animal need a way of getting around. If AIDS was, as are the really contagious diseases, effectively "air-borne" in the tiny droplets of water expelled when we sneeze, or capable of transmission from person to person through hand-shaking, most of us would now be dead. But its mode of infection is, luckily but poignantly, practically restricted to the intimate contact between persons that normally occurs only in sexual activity. It is primarily a sexually transmitted disease (STD), effectively limited to blood or blood-like fluids such as semen or vaginal secretions, and must mainly depend upon sexual intercourse for its spread. (The "primarily" and "normally" qualifications are in place because there are other special settings in which body fluids can possibly be exchanged, such as sharing intravenous needles or in surgery). Study of the avenues and modes of infection in a population is called epidemiology, and in the case of AIDS, it has taken on enormous significance.

This is because, first of all and most importantly, in the absence of any cure or vaccine, society's first line of defence against AIDS must be preventing the infection of those who don't have it, and effective prevention depends upon knowing how the disease is spreading itself. In the case of a really deadly disease that can be fairly readily protected against by individuals who know what to do, epidemiology is of the essence. Although there is a limit to the usefulness of the comparison, the epidemiological study of a disease is like the study of the spread of a city fire. Where, when, and how did it start? how is it being spread? where is it now? where will it be next? what sorts of buildings or neighborhoods are most at risk? if we can't save the buildings that are already burning, how do we stop or slow the involvement of others? And finally, of course, what should we tell people to do?

This consideration brings us to a point at which the medical and political stories of AIDS become inextricably intertwined. As an STD, AIDS would seem to fall under the provisions of those public health laws that are in place to control the spread of such diseases. Such laws typically provide public health authorities with two sorts of powers – one of them with an epidemiological thrust, and the other with a medical purpose. The medical part of STD laws is, in this age of broad-spectrum antibiotics, simplicity itself: if you've got an STD, you are legally obligated to submit to treatment so that you can't continue to spread the disease. The epidemiological thrust of the laws is connected with the need to precisely locate the disease by using what we know – here's a person with VD – in order to find out what we need to know – who else has got it? The logical thing to do is exactly what STD laws require of those infected persons who come to the knowledge of public health authorities: provide as much information as possible about the names and locations of those persons with whom they have had sexual contact. Those contacts are then required to submit to testing for the STD, with treatment and further contact tracing following along if they've got it too. Obviously, there are very important civil rights concerns raised by such legally mandated contact tracing, and they are usually addressed within the law by strict provisions for the maintenance of confidentiality or anonymity by public health authorities. In general, however, such unusual limitations of individual freedom and privacy have been justified by a clear, vital, and attainable public health interest.

This is where the paths of AIDS policy and ordinary public health law diverged. In general, throughout North America, STD laws were not applied to AIDS. This seemed remarkable – if not positively criminal to many – who reasoned that in the case of a catastrophic illness, the protection of public health interests aimed at by such laws ought to be most vigorously pursued with them. Many grumbled that government was afraid of gays or "soft" on them. (The Civil Liberties Association persuaded the city council of Vancouver to support our lobby with the provincial government to enact anti-discrimination legislation covering AIDS people, and to put in place protections for AIDS people working for the city. At the council meeting at which our initiative finally passed, a very conservative and colorful alderman leaned over to me and said – before quitting the chamber with a flourish for the TV cameras – "I hope you .... live long enough to see the consequences of what you've done here today.")

Nevertheless, there were good reasons for setting aside the powers of the STD laws in the case of AIDS, and they had nothing to do with the sexual sympathies of policy-makers. They had, rather, everything to do with results. It is important to understand this point, since finally, as I will argue later, it bears on the issue of the governance of therapies.

The argument stood on two legs. First of all, AIDS was different from the STDs that were controlled by public health laws, because there was absolutely no treatment to offer or impose upon the infectious. The only way to ensure that an AIDS person could not possibly infect others (that is, with a degree of certainty analogous to that obtainable by imposing antibiotic treatment on someone who had VD), would be to quarantine them, which would be at once unjust (since it would be predicated upon the invidious assumption that those infectious with AIDS were remarkably irresponsible) and impractical (since the numbers of people at issue were huge). Secondly, Persons With Aids were peculiarly susceptible to discriminatory treatment because of widespread and hysteria-fostering ignorance concerning the limited modes of infection of the disease, and also because most of those who had it were members of a minority that was already generally despised. Many policy-makers feared being stampeded into the (maybe) politically attractive but terribly unjust course of quarantine (which the application of STD laws could be seen as a first step towards), and they feared it not simply out of common humanity, but out of regard for the protection of public health.

Because there was a threat from the other side. If contact tracing and mandatory testing were imposed, both those who were infectious and those who feared that they were infectious would be driven underground. STD laws work on the presumption that we get control of the infection when we get control of the infectious who come forward for treatment and testing. Rather than expose themselves and their fellows to unjust treatment, those who feared that they were infected with AIDS would simply refuse to come forward and cooperate with public health authorities. To which some public-policy experts responded: "So let 'em. They'll be driven to come to us sooner or later for treatment, whether they like it or not."

That response (predicated on the notion that the infectious would prove to be as visible a minority as, say, the Japanese were in North America during the Second World War) was foolish, and the explanation of its error takes us back to the heart of the medical story. The crux of the matter is the variable, but generally considerable period of time in which a person infected with HIV (a "seropositive individual": that is, a person whose blood serum tests positive for the presence of antibodies to the AIDS virus) continues to feel perfectly well – indeed, suffers from no symptoms whatsoever (and hence is termed, through this incubation period, an "asymptomatic seropositive"). The outside limits of this period are still unknown, but the evidence in early 1990 supports an estimate of anywhere from one month to twenty years, with the mean period being about nine to ten years. Asymptomatic seropositives are infectious, and can pass on their disease to anyone with whom they have unsafe or unprotected contact.

So the notion that the infectious would be driven into the

waiting arms of public health authorities by the need for treatment flew in the face of the medical facts. True, *eventually* the illness of PWAs could be expected to make them emerge aboveground, but reaching them so late would be next to useless for controlling the spread of their disease. Much, and probably most, of the infectious life-span of PWAs would be asymptomatic, and if they didn't know they were infectious, they would be much more likely to infect others than if they did know their "HIV status." This supposition was grounded in the rather solid and commonsensical idea that any moderately decent human beings who knew they could pass on a deadly and incurable disease to others would be much more likely to act so as to prevent that happening than if they didn't know that they were infectious. Clearly, the most dangerous possibility was a state of affairs in which there was a significant number of infectious carriers of the disease living and acting in ignorance of their condition.

Pondering this, some policy makers suggested immediate and widespread mandatory testing, with a view to locating as many of the infectious as possible. The idea here was to neutralize the "threat" of the infectious to go underground (never voiced by them as such, but predicted by some of their advocates) by casting the epidemiological net as wide and deep as possible right away. Reflection revealed this to be yet another bad idea.

First of all, there was the practical matter of how wide and how deep to cast the net. An absolutely general test of the entire population would be, at once, hopelessly expensive and stupidly wasteful of limited public health-care resources. It simply didn't make any medical sense to be drawing blood from the chaste denizens of old-age homes on the expensive off-chance that they were seropositive. But a focused program of mandatory testing – i.e. one that went to where we knew the action was, in the gay community – was, besides raising all sorts of vexing civil rights questions, clearly doomed to failure as an effective public health strategy. The problem was that although we obviously knew where a lot of gays were to be found, we just as obviously did not know where all of them were. And when one reflected for a moment about the difficulties involved in focusing a mandatory testing program on bisexuals, a group diffused throughout the "straight-acting, straight-appearing" community (to quote a phrase used by this group as they seek out one another in personal ads), one understood that the notion of focusing a mandatory testing program was an illusory one. There were, as well, all sorts of difficulties with the available – i.e. affordable – tests, which, to cut a long technical story short, were all too likely to give a false result one way or the other.

But the greatest difficulty with the idea of a focused program of mandatory testing stemmed from the supposed ultimate object of the exercise. Let us say, at a wildly optimistic guess, that we could find 60 or even 75 percent of the seropositives right now by the vigorous exercise of enormous quantities of governmental muscle and treasure. Now what? When you make a big effort to chase after people and catch them, the usual idea is that you then do something to make it all worth your while. Quarantine? In the first instance, the sheer numbers involved in North America by the time anyone was thinking along these lines were already so staggering as to make quarantine a practical impossibility. It was a dream for some, and a nightmare for others, but preventative quarantine of the HIV infectious was never a realistic option in the West. So if not quarantine, then what? The answer was, of course, counselling, a measure of medical superintendence of the development of the illness in infected individuals, and the trial of promising therapies. But in any case, not the sort of denouement ordinarily associated with the close of a successful chase.

Which raised the very salient point of the state of mind of those caught in a huge program of mandatory testing, and, even more importantly, the state of mind of that infectious (and very numerous) group of individuals who slipped through the net. They could be expected to be much more frightened and resentful than they would otherwise be. That is, they would be in precisely the state of mind to make a program of prevention that depended upon their cooperative trust less likely to succeed.

Thus, if "getting tough" with them once we found them wasn't on, then widespread mandatory testing had to be abandoned as a counter-productive strategy.

This conclusion was supported from yet another perspective when one asked and answered a basic epidemiological question: who was most likely to know the identity of those individuals who were most at risk for HIV infection, and for whom testing was an important part of a comprehensive public health effort? The answer is, of course, those very individuals themselves – possessing personal and complete knowledge of their history of risk behaviour. And with that answer, the very substantial advantages of a completely voluntary program of testing, supported by the most carefully crafted and scrupulously administered standards of confidentiality or anonymity, became abundantly apparent. Such a program made it possible for us to use one of the few things we had going for us in our efforts to locate the people we needed to find: they, at least, already knew who they were. If we spent our public-health dollars in a practically useless program of quarantine of the infectious, we could expect much less return on our investment in the effort to engage the cooperative trust of this group.

So we made an exception of AIDS where STD public health laws were concerned, and got on with what must surely be the most intensive public health educational effort in history. There is, of course, a much bigger and more complex story to be told about all of the marginal skirmishes that were fought out around this issue in what might be called the "You Can't Get It That Way" educational struggles, but it is important to see that the central features of the mandatory testing question, and its resolution, were rooted in the specific and special medical features of AIDS along with the fact that when AIDS came to North America, it came for a minority that had been pre-defined by characteristics that had nothing to do with this disease.

It is important to note that the mandatory testing issue was not settled on a "rights" basis. It is true that some efforts were made to argue for a right to exclusion from such testing, but I do not think that they were well conceived. The most common argument encountered was the one which claimed, as its major premise, that since AIDS was typically contracted through sexual activity, and sexual activity was typically consensual, it was "the disease that you didn't have to get." Leaning on the minor premise that government had no business with the voluntary activities of adults in the bedrooms of the nation, the conclusion was drawn that government had no legitimate role to play in governing AIDS through such an intrusive instrument as mandatory testing. The underlying idea here was that since those who caught AIDS in the late Eighties did so, typically, with their eyes wide open, the prevention of further transmission was properly seen as the business of individuals – and perhaps their immediate communities – rather than the business of government.

The fatal weakness of this argument is that, although it is true that AIDS is a disease which individual citizens need not get, it is also sadly predictable that very many of us will go on to get it anyway. A sexually transmissible disease is a disease with very long legs under it. Recognizing this, government is not reasonably dissuaded from governing AIDS because its principal opportunity of transmission is through an activity for which we ordinarily provide a range of privacy rights. The public interest stakes at issue in the fight against AIDS are extremely high, and if widespread mandatory testing could plausibly contribute to an effective public health program against the disease, government would be justified in over-riding some privacy rights to pursue it.

It is worth noting, in passing, that the "AIDS is the disease you don't have to get" truth has had two thoroughly foolish inferences drawn from it. Some activists in the gay community argued that it is wrong for those who know their HIV status (whether positive or negative) to reveal it to those with whom they engage in sex. The idea here was that refusing to reveal this information would underscore the shared responsibility for preventing transmission in a mutually consensual sexual act, and thus further the political argument against testing. But since it is so obvious that persons will be much more cautious in the presence of a real, identified, and present danger than a theoretical and probably absent one, this line was a P.R. disaster for the gay community. Most unfortunately, it reinforced a straight stereotype of gays as a group for whom sex came first and everything else – like moral scruples and civic responsibility – a bad third.

The other foolish construction on the "you don't have to get it" line comes from the straight community, and it is the idea that "AIDS is a self-inflicted wound." The corollary is, of course, "you want to be left alone? you've got it." In B.C., two cabinet ministers (one of them the Minister of Health!) have recently offered this reflection, or one of its variants, in public. This attitude betrays, in my view, a conception of human sexuality that is – in the context of AIDS – at once astonishingly unsophisticated and politically irresponsible. Let me put it simply and directly: we aren't built to see the body of the beloved as a pit of contagion, and it is very difficult for us to take prophylactic steps which introduce such an inferred possibility into the tender moments of our love lives. Of course, sexual self-control tends to improve a lot in late middle-age, and cabinet ministers may be reasonably expected to have their fair share of this bonus of the aging process. But the young, for whom they have a heavy responsibility, do not, and it is for these that they must both imagine and govern.

Taking a balanced view of the related facts – that sex is at once among our most urgent motives, and yet squarely within the range of behaviour over which we can exercise control and choice – isn't easy. When these difficult considerations are freighted with the dangers of AIDS, balance becomes more difficult still. Of some help is the spectacle of the policy errors of others. In the Soviet Union many, if not all, HIV infected individuals who come to the knowledge of officials are reported to have been very strictly quarantined or actually imprisoned. If this is true, it is a disgraceful commentary on the confidence of the Soviet people in their socialistic talent for bringing individual responsibility to bear on a community crisis. For Westerners, the relevant consideration has been the flip side of the "you don't have to get it" slogan, which is that "you don't have to *give* it."

Once one recognizes this, and joins it to the realization that those who are most likely to be infected with AIDS are at least known to themselves if not to public health authorities, one sees the wisdom of basing the fight against this disease in a policy of mutual trust between society and the infectious – both because we ought to, and because we must.

We can turn now to a brief consideration of the treatments for AIDS and its related conditions. Unhappily brief, as it turns out, since there is so little to tell about therapies that either work or show definite promise of working. There is, first of all, the moderately effective treatment of the Burroughs-Wellcome company called AZT or Zidovudine. It seems unlikely that AZT is going to save the lives of any PWAs, but it has a proven track record, in those who can tolerate it, of substantially lengthening and improving lives. In its present regimens of use, AZT has several very dangerous side-effects, making it more like those very special medicines we term "chemotherapies" than an ordinary drug, and you wouldn't take it on a bet unless you were trying to escape something catastrophic – like AIDS. Still, if you are a young person, an increased and usable life-span of several years can mean real hope that something better will be found in the interval, and the possibility of sustaining hope might very well be worth an extra year in itself. So you swallow your AZT and hope.

Sooner or later, however, every PWA's medical battle must centre on the characteristic opportunistic illnesses that finally win the war – the exotic cancers, wasting respiratory diseases, and intestinal parasites that led Africans to call AIDS "slim" disease. In the case of the cancers, we bring to bear all of the expertise we have in the treatment of these diseases in general, which isn't a lot. In AIDS patients, it can never be enough, since they bring no personal resources to the battle, no immune capacities to throw into the fray. The progress against the respiratory diseases of AIDS, such as pneumocystis, has been more successful. One treatment in particular – aerosolized pentamidine – has proven to be, especially when used preventively, very effective in staving off the widespread destruction of lung tissue associated with a really serious bout of pneumocystis. This could possibly lead, given the pre-eminence of pneumocystis as an AIDS-related cause of death, to as great a gain in life-span for PWAs as has AZT.

With the very important and significant exception of AZT, there is virtually no other scientifically proven anti-HIV therapy, and there are but few effective therapies for the opportunistic infections of AIDS itself. (It is too early to tell, in early 1990, but it appears that the experimental drug DDI is far more likely to supplement than supplant AZT in the frontline of anti-viral therapy.) This fact reminds PWAs of a very troubling feature of the analogy I drew earlier between a city fire and the epidemic. I pointed out, in describing the work of epidemiology, that if we couldn't save the buildings that were already burning, we would have to concentrate on saving the ones that were left. One of the limitations of this analogy is that PWAs aren't just a material asset comprised of cement, steel, and wood, but are human beings – people in the kind of spot that ought to make for comparisons not with burning buildings, but with kids stuck at the bottom of a well. They don't want to be left on the wrong side of a fire-line dug between them and everybody else.

Which brings us naturally back to the matter at hand, which is the claim of PWAs that their special circumstances give them a greater than ordinary right to obtain and use experimental drugs. We turn now to this special issue.

II
Cheaters and Rebels

THE ISSUE of freedom of access to experimental drugs was dramatically, if unintentionally, posed by an edition of *Dimensions*, the special newspaper of the Fifth International Conference on AIDS in Montreal.

The June 7 1989 issue of the paper carried, on page three, a story reporting the findings of Dr. Margaret Fischl, of the University of Miami School of Medicine, concerning the importance of early treatment of AIDS with AZT. Fischl found that the greatest impact of AZT occurs during the first six to eighteen months of treatment, and the greatest effect is on patients with the first signs of AIDS symptoms in AIDS Related Complex (ARC). The same article reported the findings of Dr. Douglas Richman and his co-workers of the University of California, who found a ten-fold increase in resistance to AZT in patients who had received the drug for six to twelve months. The clear implication of this article was that, in HIV infection, early intervention with anti-virals may be vital, and that the earliest possible intervention in asymptomatic seropositives was a logically compelling option to explore.

But if HIV infected persons at the conference took the findings of Fischl and Richman "personally," that is, as information important to their individual choices and actions as they sought treatment, *Dimensions* had a page one story on June 7 that struck a discordant note.

"Conventional Use of Investigational Drugs Jeopardizing Controlled Studies" was the headline of the story, which began: "Dr. Ian Weller warned at Tuesday's plenary session that the use of investigational drugs as conventional treatment and the practice of preventative treatment in asymptomatic individuals was making it increasingly difficult to judge accurately the efficacy of new drugs." Dr. Weller, who was from the University College and Middlesex School of Medicine in the U.K., emphasized that "he was not speaking only for himself, but was presenting a consensus opinion derived from consultations taken over the last months with colleagues in several countries." All of these scientists were worried about the emergence of a research environment which threatened to become patient-driven rather than effectively controlled by the scientific and political elements of the therapeutic system. AIDS drugs were becoming ungovernable.

What was happening was precisely what one would expect rational PWAs to do in the face of even the rumour of findings such as were formally reported by Fischl and Richman at the conference. Realizing that AZT may have a limited window of opportunity through which to attack AIDS before the disease developed a resistance to the treatment, both the sick and the "worried well" were trying to beat their deadly foe to the punch.

Many PWAs and their supporters at the Montreal Conference wore *Silence = Death* lapel buttons, and they were speedily feeding news of the latest findings into their international network of patient coalitions and "buyers clubs." More HIV infected individuals would soon be practicing "preventative treatment" in an effort to save their lives, thus disqualifying themselves as subjects for any controlled and blinded experiment of this new therapeutic option. What is more and potentially worse, subjects in ongoing trials would be more likely to "cheat," i.e. to take extra or unapproved drugs without telling the investigators, and thus compromise the experiment. This has already become a bigger problem with subjects in trials of AIDS drugs than medical scientists have ever experienced with any other group.

But before we go any further, some comment on experimentation is in order. An experiment is an "essay" or "try" in which one actually does something with a view to closely observing the results. Experimentation is such a powerful tool for gathering knowledge because it is an activity which gives focused point to the attention of the seeker, making it possible to wring out the most efficient use of our necessarily limited intelligence. In this respect, one is reminded of the old cartoon of a vulture commenting laconically to one of his companions that "if nothing happens soon, I'm going to go out and kill something." Experimental investigators make things happen so that they know both where and when to look for "looked for" (i.e. hypothesized) results. Without experimentation, there is a sense in which one waits always and watches everywhere, and although a very intelligent observer of nature can do much under such circumstances (Newton under his apple tree comes to mind – though Einstein would have called this a "thought experiment"), it is generally wasteful of the resources of both the strongest and the weakest minds.

Beyond this sovereign feature of planned intellectual activity, experimentation has also provided the necessary basis for verifying results by the repetition of experiments by the same or other investigators, thus partially realizing the elusive ideal of observer neutrality (one of the essential conditions for objectivity). What is more, the standardized recording and communication of experiments and their results has culminated in the creation of one of humankind's greatest and most enduring achievements – the scientific community. That intellectual community has become, quite simply, a synonym for syncretic power.

Much as every figure has a background, every experimental result has a state of affairs against which it stands out, and with which it is compared. The simplest instance of this takes the form of comparing the result of your activity with what would have been the case had you done nothing. One releases the apple from the hand, and observes that . . . and what one observes can be cleanly and unequivocally compared with the certain knowledge of what would have happened if you had held on to it. This elegant simplicity is lost, however, the moment one ventures into the region of unknown or imperfectly known phenomena. Thus, the ultimate cautionary tale of science, concerning the Ancient Chinese and eclipses of the sun. As the story goes, the Chinese rushed to the temple at every eclipse, and banged away on a sacred gong in order to scare away whatever monster was engulfing the life-giving orb. The "result" of this "experiment" was always the same – the monster relented and the eclipse was ended. As for what would have happened if the priests had failed to gong the monster? No one among those ancients dared risk making such an observation.

Their problem was, as any school-child among us could tell them, that they were operating on a *presumed* account of what would have been the case if they had not gonged, and this presumption led them to misconstrue their results. Their experiment stood in need of a specific and special effort to establish what would have happened without their intervention, which is to say, in scientific parlance, that their experiment needed a control to exclude the variable of an unlooked-for heavenly body both causing and ending the eclipse.

This business of controls is of special significance in medical experimentation, since one of the successes of modern medicine is that it has vanquished many of the diseases for which we possessed a reasonably complete "natural history" (the whole medical, clinical, and epidemiological story of the course of the disease in an untreated individual or group of individuals). Thus, researchers are often experimenting with treatments for diseases in which there are such large areas of ignorance that they could not say with certainty what would happen if they did nothing. Moreover, there are a range of human variables involved in treatment which must be controlled. Both the conscious and unconscious expectations of physicians and patients are powerfully engaged by the administration of medicine, and their effects on observed results can be so significant as to over-shadow the specific action of the tested drug.

Finally, and most significantly among the infectious diseases, there are the variables introduced by the development of resistance, which can often only be unmasked in the context of very carefully designed and controlled experiments. The mutation of the AIDS virus, which, like so many other commonplace features of this disease, was treated to front-page coverage, was the entirely expected development of a range of resistances to both natural and medical anti-viral agents. Disease viruses live a dangerous life of cat and mouse with the immune systems of their hosts, as well as with the pharmaceutical weapons of modern medicine. Their very tough environment is a ruthlessly selective one, and a viral agent that flourishes is one whose outer coating undergoes enough mutation to allow it to keep an unrecognized version of itself one step ahead of its natural and contrived enemies. Indeed, it might well be said that a non-mutating viral disease is a contradiction in terms; it would perish so quickly as never to enjoy identification as a threat by medical researchers. This is the difficulty of relying upon "historical" controls, i.e. the record of the medical progress of some past control group in some other study, or a meticulously gathered set of medical histories from the records of primary-care physicians. With the passage of time, we might be dealing with a disease that has changed in ways that are critical to the centrally relevant medical issue – how do we successfully treat it *now*?

Beyond these considerations, the case for experimental controls is strengthened when one recognizes that a significant improvement in treatment might still be small enough to escape recognition against the background of an imperfect grasp of the natural history of a disease. This refers back to the point emphasized by Dr. Weller in Montreal when he complained of the increasing difficulty involved for investigators who are carefully attending, not simply to some gross result such as can be captured by noticing whether or not the subject is still alive, but who must judge accurately the appearance of conditions that may only indirectly suggest an improvement ("surrogate markers" in the jargon). Such subtle effects of treatment might, of course, escape investigators even in a controlled setting, but the best chance of catching a slight but significant effect (which could lead to other hypotheses and experiments which build on that knowledge) is in the most carefully controlled setting possible.

Thus, the "gold standard" of protocols in drug research – as Robert Levine of Yale argued at the Montreal Conference – is the double-blinded, randomized experiment. In its classic simplicity, this involves the inclusion of only those subjects who satisfy a carefully predetermined standard of relevant homogeneity – i.e. all with about the same stage of disease development, same history of treatment or non-treatment, etc. – and then their separation into two distinct arms. One group of subjects receives the experimental drug, and is called the experimental arm. The other group of subjects receives the control substance (either a placebo or the established therapy), and is called the control arm. The experiment is randomized in that the selection of subjects for the different arms is made as perfectly random as possible in order to control such possible human variables as, say, an investigator unconsciously placing the most likable subjects in the experimental arm. And it is double-blinded in that it is arranged so that neither the investigators nor the subjects know who is in which arm, thus controlling the range of human variables associated with expectation and hope.

Obviously, subject compliance or discipline is an important consideration in such experimentation. For if subjects figure out which arm they are in, or take drugs other than those controlled for by the experimental design, the results can be compromised (i.e. there may be effects observed that are not attributable to the experimental drug, but to uncontrolled variables), and at least a portion of the scientific objective lost.

Which brings us back to the issue of "cheating" subjects in the trial of drugs for AIDS. In the United States, it is said that a significant number of subjects in the first phase of human trials of AZT agreed among themselves to pool the medications dispensed to them by the scientific investigators. The idea was to guarantee every one in the bargain that even if they had been randomized into the control arm (which was receiving a placebo in that trial), they would stand an even chance of receiving an approximate half-dose of AZT. To the extent that these "pill parties" actually happened – unsurprisingly, there is no documentation – they compromised the experiment both by introducing large dosage variables, and by significantly weakening the controlling function of the control arm. Investigators tore their hair out, but there was little they could do to prevent it.

There were several factors working against the scientifically important factor of subject discipline in this AZT trial. First of all, scientific life becomes much more complicated when we descend from the level of pure theory and practice of animal experimentation to the field of research on human subjects. For openers, there is an obvious sense in which the maintenance of either subject or investigator blindness in the trial of powerful drugs is problematical – if not impossible. For while blindness can be mechanically or administratively *created*, its *maintenance* in human experimentation requires a very real degree of clinical naiveté – a trait hopefully absent in medical investigators, and notably absent in highly motivated patients such as PWAs. If, to put it crudely, the medical journals tell us that dose "b" of drug "X" causes your hair to fall out within two weeks, nobody in the experimental arm of a trial of "X" is going to fail to realize that they aren't taking a placebo, and both the investigators and well-read subjects are going to have a very good idea of what is happening. There is, in all of the real situations in which blindness is subtly compromised, an obvious incentive for investigators to avoid noticing what is going on. They have a big stake in the scientific credentials of their experiment. This isn't scientific or any other kind of villainy, but just good old human nature doing its thing. However, quite the opposite set of natural forces is at work in a set of catastrophically ill subjects. Their minds are wonderfully concentrated on the matter at hand, which is survival or, at least, the warding off of proximate death. Many of the subjects in both arms of the AZT trial knew what to look for in order to determine what they were on, and they had an incentive to look.

The incentive was, besides the liveliest form of interested personal curiosity, the possibility of saving lives – both their own and others. Many PWAs were convinced that the placebo-controlled trial of AZT was immoral, given the existing anecdotal evidence concerning efficacy (real but limited), and toxicity (variable but possibly intolerable) from the preliminary human trials. So they compromised the experiment and, as it scientifically turns out (recalling again the results of Fischl and Richman presented at Montreal), probably succeeded in at least temporarily saving the lives of a considerable number of people.

We should not delude ourselves that every, or even many such initiatives on the part of non-compliant research subjects ends happily. The point of this anecdote is not to establish such a misleading impression, or to encourage rebellion. But it is important to see that the controversy over access to experimental drugs is not just a little fuss over principle or semantics. Momentous human stakes are being fought over within it, and some very bitter feelings have developed on both sides. Researchers feel betrayed, and the idea that they are dealing with "cheaters" who can't be trusted to keep their word is becoming more general. They point out – for the millionth time, judging by the exasperation in most of their voices – that experimentation is most definitely *not* treatment, that experimental subjects must ("and do, or at least they *said* that they did") understand that critical difference. A volunteer for such drug trials is a *volunteer*: "nobody put a gun to their heads."

To this the catastrophically ill point out that there is no need for anybody to put a gun to their head in order to extract a desperate compliance to the conditions of placebo-controlled experiment – where they stand only a 50 percent chance of getting the drug that they want. They already have a gun to their head in the form of their prognosis. If they want even the small hope afforded them by an untested drug, they must take what is permitted to them by the therapeutic authorities. Hence, as they would have it, they enter into the same kind of "voluntary" undertakings as do the starving poor of Calcutta, who search out the opportunity to sell enough of their blood to ensure both the temporary survival of their families, and their own probable death. Nobody has to bring coercion to them; they bring their own to be taken advantage of. In such circumstances we should, they contend, speak not of "cheaters" but of "rebels."

So there are at least two deeply divided perspectives on this issue, and two sets of conflicting claims to go with them. Neither of them is frivolous. The first is that of the catastrophically ill patients, facing death and determined to avoid or forestall it, and the second is that of what I will call the "therapeutic authorities" – the research community and officials of government, joined loosely with the management of the pharmaceutical companies – who must plan and act not only out of the exigencies of a desperate and personalized present, but with a view to discharging their obligations to society in general and over time. There is here, in a phrase, a clash between private and social; between a claim of individual rights and the demands of serving the public interest.

It is obvious that these claims do not lend themselves to any simple reconciliation, and that their relative merits must be adjudicated, either explicitly or implicitly, by those responsible for public policy. The point of this essay is to offer a framework for the provision of justice in this very difficult setting. The framework involves that which may be viewed with philosophical suspicion – the introduction of a novel individual prerogative, which I am calling a "catastrophic right." However, the account I propose here has the saving virtue of describing that catastrophic right in terms of its symmetry with what is perhaps the most established of all patients' rights in the democracies – the right to refuse medical treatment. And, although the language of rights can lend itself to war-cries, I will argue that it can also help us place the access to experimental treatment problem on terrain that is already fairly well mapped in our moral and legal tradition. This makes it possible not only to measure the force and extent of catastrophic rights, but also to establish their limits.

III.
Standard
Operating
Procedure

THE CATASTROPHICALLY ill confront, with their claim of a special individual right, a world with a long-established policy goal of protecting public health interests by controlling the use of medicines. Any attempt to introduce a novel right in this area should begin with a consideration of the range of public interests that are and have been, as a matter of general policy, sought and obtained by the therapeutic authorities of society. First the ordinary, then the special.

There are at least three overlapping categories of such ordinary and general public interests: the protection of people, the conservation of health-care resources, and the maintenance of our ability to do science.

The protection
of people

JUST AS we do not have to take complete individual responsibility for determining the quality and wholesomeness of the canned tuna we buy at the corner store, we can expect that the drugs sold by our pharmacist have been judged safe and effective by the Federal Government. We take this for granted until we travel to other jurisdictions in which a visit to the drug store can be a many-splendored and dangerous consumer outing – giving fresh meaning to the invitation to "shop until you drop." The provision of such regulatory protection is a form of paternalism, a limitation of the freedom of persons "for their own good." Some libertarian thinkers find such governmental paternalism to be obnoxious to the very idea of democracy. They argue that if The People are wise enough to be entrusted with the ultimate political authority in our system of government, then they must, consistent with that central and fundamental ideal, be given sovereignty over the less important matter of their individual therapeutic fates as well.

This is not the place to engage the absolutist democratic opposition to governmental paternalism, but I would observe that the regulation of the sale of drugs provides an enormous measure of convenience as well as safety to all citizens, and is perhaps a vital protection for the very many helpless and credulous among us. Generally speaking, we are less able to marshall our ordinary abilities to care for ourselves when we are ill, and the more seriously ill, the more attenuated our general powers become. Thus the paternalistic control of therapies is an important benefit in that it protects us from dangers at the specific point at which we would be most susceptible to them. When we consider the importance of consent to medical treatment being informed (because if not informed, then it isn't genuinely voluntary), and then reflect upon the often desperate and distracted condition of the ill, it is easy to appreciate the value of at least some regulatory protection from the blandishments of snake-oil salesmen. If this, as an element of general policy in dealing with ordinary illness, poses some slight threat to the vitality of our democratic freedoms – an arguable contention – it has paid off that cost in such substantial and proven benefits that its status as general policy is, as a practical matter, as beyond reconsideration as is the non-paternalistic regulation of aircraft maintenance and pork-chops.

Apart from the paternalistic protection of patients, the therapeutic authorities have yet another protective agenda in the special case of infectious or communicable diseases. People with infectious diseases have something that goes beyond "their own business." Although the recognition of this does not change the fact that they should have a central role to play in the "minding" of it, the rest of us have a stake in its management or mismanagement as well. The control and extirpation of such diseases are of vital importance in the protection of public health, and there are a range of public health measures that are uncontroversially associated with the attainment of this legitimate public purpose. Whether the governance of experimentation with catastrophic therapies belongs among these measures is a question we will return to later.

Finally, there is, in connection with the public interest in protecting persons, the consideration that society must discharge its responsibility not only to those who presently have a disease, but to those of its members who may get it in the future. This provides a reason for limiting the therapeutic autonomy of individual patients that is quite distinct from the paternalistic ones. We may need to sacrifice a measure of their individual freedom to a public and social purpose that involves persons who are not yet even born.

The conservation of limited health-care resources

THE POWER of our therapeutic system is intimately linked with the power of our medicines. To the extent that we have and use safe and effective drugs to treat the sick, there is proportionally less consumption of our limited ability to palliate and maintain them. And to the extent that we have and use safe and effective palliative and maintaining treatments when, as is too often true, we cannot cure, we have more resources left with which to turn to those most demanding cases for which we have no such medicines.

Beyond saving people from and for themselves, there is the consideration of who will end up paying for their mistakes, if and when they choose to use drugs that are neither safe nor effective. Thus, a government which recognizes a responsibility to conserve limited health-care resources will pursue a limited paternalism which regulates the commercial sale of drugs in terms of the expert community's judgment of their safety and efficacy. There can be little doubt that the "discipline of the marketplace" would, if permitted to operate in this arena as it does in others, provide a real measure of self-regulation of the consumption of health-care resources. But there can be even less doubt that while North Americans either enjoy or are inured to the rough-and-tumble discipline inseparable from "freedom of choice!" on the used-car lot, they would regard its completely unfettered operation in the sick-room as a cruelty that should be avoided by the application of a rational governance.

The May 15 1989 *Time* magazine reported that both Oregon and California were moving in the direction of rationing health care with a view to curbing, with strict attention to fairness, the seemingly endless expansion of public costs associated with the treatment of serious illness. The move was heralded by many experts, including Daniel Callahan, director of the prestigious Hastings Center, one of the most important centers for the study of bioethical issues. As *Time* reported his comments:

> Trying to contain medical costs by greater efficiencies is "wishful thinking" in his view. One reason is the inexorable aging of America, as the nation's over-65 population rises from about 28 million today to a projected 35 million by the year 2000. Callahan also blames high-tech research for producing ingenious new operations that remain astronomically pricey even as they become popular and desirable. He proposes a slowdown on developing gimmicky procedures like artificial hearts and a more careful review of their social and economic consequences. Says he: "We keep inventing new ways to spend money, and that complicates things."
>
> *Time* May 15, 1989.

The emergence of this new argument for government restrictions on the consumption of health care militates even more strongly against the indulgence of therapies which have *not* been proven, to the satisfaction of the therapeutic authorities, to be either safe or effective. Of course, the emergence of such policies, and Callahan's positive commentary upon them, must always be seen against the background consideration of the "greying" of the populations of the West. At the risk of putting the matter crudely: if there are limited resources available with which to accomplish the task of medical salvation, it makes sense to invest more heavily in the saving of very young lives than the saving of very old ones. Still, one person's gimmick is another person's life-saver. We will return to these considerations later.

The maintenance
of our ability
to do science

THIS SEEMINGLY abstract notion has enormous practical importance in connection with questions of public health interests versus individual freedom because, as we have already seen, the genuinely *scientific* determination of the safety and efficacy of experimental drugs depends upon carefully controlled study of their effects. If we are to have medical progress, we must have knowledge; if we are to have knowledge, we must have science; and if we are to have science, we must have experimental controls. Unhappily, the antiseptic notion of control of studies necessarily translates into the troubling reality of the control of persons.

As a general consideration, however, this instance of society getting organized around a communal purpose is clearly just another good idea at work rather than a dramatic slice of "civilization and its discontents." Consider, for instance, all of the people who suffer from migraine headaches (as many as 15 percent of North Americans by some reports). Each of these individual sufferers has a pressing individual interest in obtaining fast relief, and each will certainly be inclined to try different therapies in an effort to find something that works. If we leave the project of finding a cure for migraine to the unfettered enterprise of all of these separate individual inclinations to keep trying – joined by, of course, all of those medical entrepreneurs who will service the inclination – there is at least a logical possibility we may finally stumble on something that is safe and effective. Our practical chances of success are, however, enormously improved if we organize our effort to find a migraine cure around the established system of experimentation that is utilized by medical science. Bringing genuine and effective social organization to such a scientific effort means, however, that the ordinary freedom of persons to keep trying therapies will be limited. Getting organized translates into getting governed.

Rational migraine sufferers have to weigh the relative attractiveness of two scenarios: one in which they have a completely privatized and unfettered right to scour the earth for novel therapies for their affliction, and in which they have virtually no practical chance of success; and another in which they must relinquish a measure of their therapeutic autonomy to a social and scientific authority that will organize the search for a cure in terms of the scientific method. The latter and scientific scenario is the easy winner of this contest. It suffers, of course, from the fault of being a choice which entails a measure of paternalism. But we have, in this connection as in the instance of general consumer interests, historically accepted a very limited paternalism against the background of the very substantial benefits gained through its narrow operation. A nation without migraine is a better nation, and it is most specially a better nation for migraine sufferers. Which is one good reason among several others that we don't hear cries of "human guinea pigs!" in protest at controlled investigation of experimental headache cures.

The point to be taken from all of this is that the regulation of drugs isn't just an authoritative whim or bad habit of our governments. It is grounded in, and legitimized by, the effort to protect public health. Thus, the ordinary governance of drugs involves the regulation of those experimental protocols which are to prove safety and efficacy so as to make them consistent with the randomized, double-blinded standard. To do otherwise or less is to do less than the best science, and to take that course is to risk compromising the public health interests that are dependent upon our ability to make medical progress.

IV.
Another
Kingdom

THE CLEAR statement of a public interest is usually sufficient to set aside the interested claims of individuals, but to think it must always be so is an error grounded in the confusion of interests with rights. In our moral and legal tradition, some individual interests are given a special status as *rights* which may act, in at least some settings, as "trumps" over ordinarily dominant public interests.

For example, it is rumoured that a certain Third World Communist country tests experimental vaccines for catastrophic illnesses on those of its prison population convicted of serious criminal offences. Efficacy tests of vaccines are notoriously difficult when investigators are limited to the statistical study of voluntary subjects over a period of time long enough to yield significant results. The scientific virtues of simply injecting live pathogens into vaccinated subjects and observing the outcome are obvious, as are the public interests obtained by doing effective science quickly rather than slowly. But North Americans are appalled by any such policy, discovering in its simplistic weighing of public against individual interests a tyrannical disregard for the rights of the coerced experimental subjects.

I offer this extreme case, not as a pretended analogy to the issue before us, but as illustrative of the fact that where claims of individual rights – as opposed to mere individual interests – are involved, the establishment of a substantial public interest does not automatically resolve conflict; indeed, it may simply set the stage for it.

Thus, as we maintain a firm grip on the important public health interests involved, we turn to the special case for catastrophic rights urged by AIDS people. Although it represents yet another slight digression, it is necessary to ask and answer the question: what is so special about AIDS in this context? Medicine has, after all, been dealing with catastrophic illness through all of its history, and there are many categories of patients whose illness is grave, and to whom we can offer no curative hope. AIDS is a "johnny-come-lately" on this somber scene.

The answer to the question is that there is absolutely nothing medically or philosophically or legally special about AIDS as a catastrophic illness. What is special about AIDS is that PWAs possess, for a complex of reasons we need not examine here, the *political* power needed to confront the therapeutic system with a case for the rights of all catastrophically ill patients. In joining these inhabitants of "Another Kingdom," they have added their very powerful voice to what has traditionally been a silent or politically disorganized constituency.

What can they fairly claim? First of all, that the catastrophically ill are set apart from the general patient population by the fact that they face, in addition to the suffering ordinarily associated with illness, the ultimate human disaster of death. (I shall not pause to argue the disastrous character of death with the naysayers – letting it stand at least for those of us who are neither believers nor, as was Job at the end, "full of years.") And secondly, that competence is a necessary condition for the justification of any paternalistic system. It is, finally, because "father knows best" that he has both the right and duty to limit the freedom of his children "for their own sake," and it is because established medicine knows best how to treat sickness that it has an authoritative role to play in governing therapy. But by the same token and logic, where the therapeutic system must admit a lack of competence, it must also admit that its ordinary authority is compromised or weakened. The catastrophically ill are, as it were, perched on a crumbling ledge over a chasm. No establishment-certified ropes can reach them, so the therapeutic authorities have less justification for limiting the freedom of such patients to try to save themselves with their own choice of uncertified rope.

Thus, we arrive at the intuition, offered by most North Americans who are asked to give a moment's reflection to the situation of the catastrophically ill, that "because they're going to die anyway, they have a right to try anything they want as long as it doesn't hurt anyone else." This intuition leaves a lot out of account – most obviously the indirect effects on others of patient-driven patterns of therapeutizing, and the rather important matter of who is going to pay for the experimentation and its effects. But it brings into account the consideration that the situation of the catastrophically ill is naturally and properly thought of in the special context of rights. This recognition of the fundamental importance to persons of the freedom to try to save their own lives, has an ancient lineage. But what sort of right is it, and how much freedom ought it to guarantee?

Addressing these questions, one is struck by how the loneliness of the catastrophically ill, relegated to Another Kingdom by our powerlessness to reach out to them with curative hope, calls to mind the situation of that other medical loner – the patient who refuses treatment. The right to refuse even established therapy is perhaps the most settled feature of patients' rights in the democracies. It is clearly rooted in the importance of individual integrity in our scheme of things, and the correlative right guaranteed to an individual adult person to secure his person by his own lights and in his own way. Indeed, we have almost a horror of the imposition of medical treatment, however well-intentioned, as a palpable invasion of personal integrity that offends our basic intuitions concerning both the foundations and objects of democratic life.

There is a significant symmetry between the well-established right of the "refusing" patient, and the novel claim for catastrophic rights. It rests in the conflict, in both instances, between an individual patient's vision of what is best for himself – rooted in a personal conception of what is

requisite to the maintenance of his life, or a religious conviction, or even a determination to die – and society's vision of what is best for everyone. And in both cases, the patient appeals to the special importance we attach to, and the special rights we provide for, the self-determination of individuals in that which affects them most personally and profoundly.

In both instances, the individual patient insists: "Count me out of your 'everyone' in this matter, where my personal fate is intimately affected and concentrated in my body itself, and by comparison with which, the 'interest of everyone' is a diffuse and bloodless idea."

The United States and Canada have a legal and moral tradition that confers a trumping value on individual integrity and autonomy over ordinarily countervailing social interests in at least some settings. The right of the refusing patient is a settled example of this democratic prejudice at work in the therapeutic situation. A patient refusing established and proven therapy typically continues to make a claim on the palliative care necessitated by their continued illness (and provided by the very medical-social system which respected the claim of an individual right by laying aside its paternalistic authority). Yet our special regard for the right of the individual to be personally active – both intellectually and practically – where the security of their own person is the central issue, outweighs the obvious social costs.

To the extent to which there is symmetry between the circumstances of the refusing and the catastrophic patient, there ought also be symmetry between the individual rights accorded them in the face of *ordinarily* over-riding public interests.

Such individual rights are clearly not absolute, and catastrophic rights should not be regarded as an all or nothing affair, or as a sort of on-off switch for patient sovereignty. Indeed, the symmetry between the refusing and catastrophic patient owes much of its significance to the fact that it locates, on fairly well-mapped and negotiable rights terrain, the demand of PWAs for a special measure of freedom to try to save themselves. Just as the symmetry gives substance and shape to catastrophic rights, it helps us judge their appropriate limits.

The symmetry between the patient claiming a right to refuse medical treatment, and the catastrophic patient claiming a right to therapeutic self-determination is limited by the difference in the response they seek from society, and also by the distribution of consequences that flow from society's honouring their respective claims. When society stands aside in the case of the refusing patient, it is asked – literally – for nothing, and the consequences of its inactivity are practically limited to the necessity of maintaining or palliating the refuser. But when society stands aside in the case of the catastrophic patient, it will be drawn into a real measure of active participation with the patient in the provision of the catastrophic treatment, and the consequences may threaten the public interests served by the social control of therapies which we have already considered. Those public interests may be diffuse and bloodless as compared with the interests of the catastrophic patient, but they are for all that real, substantial, and appropriate objects of public health policy. They should not be swept aside without careful consideration, because their protection may be of vital importance.

We noted above that the response to the refusing patient involves society in a measure of participation with them, in that we would not abandon such patients because of their decision to disagree with our therapeutic recommendations. We might incur additional and substantial health care costs as a consequence of our honouring their – presumably ill-advised – refusal of the therapy of choice. But the effects of positively responding to the right to refuse treatment are, fairly considered, of a lesser magnitude than the typical possible consequences of honouring catastrophic rights.

This asymmetry underscores a distinction between these two rights. In the case of the refusing patient, a large measure of our willingness to accede stems from the fact that the exercise of this right is one that concentrates consequences fairly narrowly on its claimants. This self-limiting characteristic is absent in the case of the claim of a catastrophic right. However, what lies at the basis of both rights is our respect for individual autonomy in that which affects us most personally and profoundly, and death is a matter of such enormous moment that its presence must always powerfully enhance the claim to autonomy of the catastrophic patient. Indeed, the right to self-preservation is "free-standing." Although the catastrophic patient asks for more than the refusing patient, he brings more to the asking.

There is another asymmetry between the refusing and the catastrophic patient, and it marks what is perhaps the most important difference in the character of the rights claimed by them. The refusing patient demands to be left alone to do what is within his competence, which is do without the ministrations he rejects. In contrast with this, the catastrophic patient demands a greater than ordinarily permitted access to that which lies within the competence and gift of others. Furthermore, and not to put too fine a point on it, when we consider that most experimental drugs are developed by pharmaceutical companies, he is demanding enhanced access to that which is owned by others. There is a big difference between wanting nothing and wanting something belonging to others, and it is this difference that forms the largest gap between the right to refuse and catastrophic rights.

The difference and gap are, however, significantly narrowed when we reflect that what both patients confront is a social and political entity, the therapeutic authorities, to which society has granted practically absolute powers over the development of medicines and the treatment of disease. The decision to permit refusal of treatment, or treatment with one drug but not with another, or to forbid treatment with the patient's choice of therapy has, by becoming a social prerogative, become a social responsibility. In our system, social authority may be curbed or limited by the legitimate claim of an individual right, and it is from this perspective that catastrophic rights are made. Still, there remains a difference between the freedoms sought by the refusing and the catastrophic patients, and we will return to a careful consideration of it when we discuss the role of the pharmaceutical companies, and the thorny issue of who pays.

Beyond these asymmetries between catastrophic rights and the rights of the refusing patient, the right to refuse is, itself, not absolute. We turn now to the most significant exceptions to the almost absolute right to refuse medical treatment in the United States and Canada, with a view to determining how they affect our modelling of catastrophic rights.

The first concerns those instances in which a patient suffering from a curable communicable disease refuses (and here we quote the phrase used by virtually all federal, provincial, and state health laws in this connection) "to conduct himself in such manner as not to expose other persons to the infection." In such instances, most often seen in cases of tuberculosis in the very poor, society must choose between the very unattractive options of the indefinite involuntary confinement of the patient or the involuntary confinement of the patient conjoined with the imposition of effective treatment just until the disease is no longer communicable. We choose the latter course, judging that it represents the least infringement of the freedom of the patient consistent with the removal of a serious threat to public health.

It is important to recognize that what lies at the bottom of this exception to the right to refuse medical treatment is the social conviction that when we *do* possess a safe and effective cure for a communicable disease, and a patient suffering from such a disease both refuses the cure and continues to wilfully or carelessly expose others to infection, we should impose treatment as the least obnoxious alternative. Such an exception is not analogous to the catastrophic situation in which there is no cure, and no good reason to suppose that the patient poses an infectious risk to the public through either malice or carelessness.

(But what should we do in those instances in which persons, either through malice or dementia, spread a disease – such as AIDS – for which there is no treatment? This question was put to me by a committee of cabinet ministers when the B.C. Civil Liberties Association lobbied them for human rights protections for the HIV infectious. My response was that the vast majority of PWAs could be expected to be just about like the rest of us in the room – decent folk who would go to great lengths to avoid infecting other people with a deadly and incurable disease. Still, there certainly exists, at the margin of the AIDS epidemic, rare individuals who could be characterized as the "malicious or demented infectious." The question for government is whether its first acts should be directed to the core of the public policy issue – reassuring the vast majority of the infectious – or to its margins, maybe scaring some of the malicious and demented, but *certainly* terrifying the very people it needs to reassure. That said, I do not believe there can be any doubt that the duty of public health authorities must be to confine the malicious infectious so as to eliminate the threat they pose to public health. This is not, of course, a "refusal of treatment" question, and the civil rights issues raised by it deserve separate treatment. In British Columbia, the BCCLA persuaded the government to amend proposed legislation which was viewed by the affected community – and the media – as a "quarantine bill." The Minister of Health finally agreed, a few days before the bill was to go before the legislature, that the definition of what constituted culpable exposure of others to disease should be tightened, and that more due process protections had to be built in. He took the unusual step of reading, in the legislature – as he introduced the new bill – the letter I wrote to him detailing the changes, and confirming that they removed the threats to civil rights posed by the original version. The story of the Bill 34 fight has been told by Stan Persky in the March-April 1988 issue of *This Magazine* in an article entitled "AIDS and the State.")

The second exception to the right to refuse treatment involves those instances in which the state intercedes to take custody of a seriously ill minor from whom the legal guardians are withholding an established therapy. Such cases, most familiar to us in the context of the religious convictions of Jehovah's Witnesses concerning blood transfusions, are not analogous to the catastrophic situation in which the patient is an adult. In the case of minors, we believe that they lack the judgment to bring genuinely informed consent to the acceptance of the consequences of refusing treatment, and the state intercedes in order to discharge its obligation to protect the incompetent. However, adult catastrophic patients are, generally, perfectly competent to understand and accept the consequences of taking a personal and active role in the determination of their therapy. In those cases in which adult patients are not competent, they are denied the right to refuse just as if they were minors.

Related to these cases, there is the very significant exclusion of the "temporarily incompetent" from the right to refuse. This is the class of patients exemplified by the newly-created quadriplegic who refuses life-sustaining treatment upon learning his diagnosis. We believe that since many of these patients may be deprived of their ordinary powers of deliberation and judgment by the shock of their fresh loss, we are justified in forcing treatment upon them for a time. Once they have adjusted to their new situation, however, they are restored to the class of competents, and we must abide by their possible decision to refuse further treatment. This strikes me as being, at least in broad outline, a reasonable way to proceed with this very special class of patients. The question then is: should we not similarly judge that the catastrophically ill are made at least partially or temporarily incompetent by their shocking prognosis? Dying patients may decide to try untested drugs as much out of desperation as calculation of the possible medical benefits. Doesn't this consideration properly motivate the imposition of a paternalistic management of their therapy?

I don't believe that paternalism is justified by these considerations, because of important differences between the temporarily incompetent and the catastrophically ill. First of all, the class of patients that characterize the temporarily incompetent are, typically, accident victims. They are in the midst of a crisis in which we are reasonably confident of medically prevailing, and we can look forward to calmer waters and smoother sailing ahead. What is more, we can ordinarily look forward to a *lifetime* of smoother sailing for the patient – a life which might well appear to him to be worth living when he contemplates it from the position of medical stability with which we can provide him. And finally, proximate death is generally not a part of the clinical picture of the temporarily incompetent. High stakes are on the table, but they are not the highest stakes, and there will be time enough to decide how to play.

All of this changes when we turn to the case of the catastrophically ill, as exemplified by AIDS patients. These patients are not properly thought of as being in the midst of the sort of medical crisis that is associated with trauma. They are more likely to be pondering their fates in a restaurant than in the recovery room of a surgical theatre. And the medical task associated with their disease is not to be thought of as the management of a disruptive storm that will give way to clear skies and clear sailing. Rather, we know that what is ahead of the catastrophic patient is the edge of his personal world. Such an irreversibly desperate medical situation may properly motivate desperate therapeutic measures, and all of the therapeutic decisions taken in this setting are for keeps. We are, therefore, considering a situation in which the case for discovering a compromised competence is much weaker, and in which momentous therapeutic choices cannot be put off. If the patient is deprived of his therapeutic autonomy, the deprivation is an irrevocable one, and hence a very serious harm to him.

Still, there is no denying that a catastrophic medical situation is genuinely desperate, and can make for desperation as easily as it can effect the "concentration of mind" spoken of by Samuel Johnson. Since desperation isn't ordinarily an aid to deliberation, concern for the state of mind which the catastrophically ill bring to their therapeutic choices shouldn't be dismissed as foolish. This is, however, the sort of consideration that can be fairly met with measures that fall far short of treating the catastrophically ill as though they were incompetent. This is an issue I will return to in the following section.

For the sake of reasonable completeness, I will at least mention forced obstetrical intervention as an exception to the right to refuse. I take it that the difference between such a controversial excepting circumstance and the typical case of the catastrophically ill is obvious. Where forced obstetrical intervention is resorted to, it is an element of a social, political, and moral commitment to the life of the unborn. That is, a judgment has been made that it is not a case in which only the life of the patient is at issue. As the pro-life faction in this controversy would have it: "every obstetrician has two patients." No such considerations enter into consideration of the therapeutic choices of the catastrophically ill.

Finally, we have the instance of enforced programs of vaccination for infectious diseases. In this case, society balances the real, calculable, but relatively minor interference with individual rights against a relatively enormous public interest – the extirpation of an infectious disease. Again, however, there are fundamental disanalogies with the typical catastrophic situation. When we override the ordinary right to refuse medical treatment in the instance of a vaccination program, we do it with the firm conviction that we possess a relatively safe and effective means of removing the threat of a serious illness not only in the case of the individual vaccinated, but from society in general. The catastrophic situation, on the other hand, has as one of its distinguishing features the fact that we lack an established therapy. Thus, the catastrophic patient is on his own as far as the resources of established medicine are concerned, and makes his claim to an enhanced right to act on his own against this background.

What all of this means, finally, is that the catastrophic patient is claiming a right that enjoys positive, but limited, symmetry with the established right to refuse treatment. And even the right to refuse has justifiable limits when it is weighed against a demonstrable, vitally important, and attainable public interest.

V.
Catastrophic Rights

PLACING ALL of these considerations in the balance, what can we say about the proper force and limits of catastrophic rights? I suggest that we move very conservatively, ascribing to catastrophic rights only the force and application which reflect their *positive* symmetry with the established right to refuse. Since, as I will argue, it turns out that even a very conservative characterization of catastrophic rights militates toward a substantial liberalization of the handling of catastrophic drugs by the therapeutic authorities, cautious and conservative movement is enough because it is plenty. In this spirit, I offer the following very general formulation as a starting point:

Catastrophic rights should be as broad as possible to reflect our respect for the claim of a special measure of therapeutic freedom for the catastrophically ill as they seek to save themselves, and they should be as narrow as is necessary to leave materially undisturbed the vital public interests served by the social control of therapy.

And how undisturbed is "materially undisturbed"? As undisturbed, I would suggest as our conservative guide, as are vital public interests when we recognize the established rights of the refusing patient. This would mean that catastrophic rights would have modest, but real, trumping force against ordinarily overriding public interests. We can usefully measure this force in the

43

context of a reconsideration of the three categories of counter-vailing public interests outlined earlier.

Paternalism
revisited

WHILE THE paternalistic governance of therapies may well make moral and legal sense in the case of ordinary illnesses, thwarting the deliberate therapeutic choices of the catastrophically ill flies in the face of the universal moral intuition that dying people ought to have more than an ordinary say in how they play their last cards. If we recognize a catastrophic right of symmetrical force and limits with the right to refuse treatment – that is, with the same narrow range of possible consequences for persons other than the patient – then whatever justification we may have for limiting the therapeutic autonomy of the catastrophically ill, it cannot be that we thwart them "for their own good." Surely, whatever their claim to be the best judge of their own interests, there can be no question that their extreme personal danger gives them the right to assess and take their own therapeutic risks. Some, and perhaps even most, may not avail themselves of such a possibility. The point about this freedom, as with most others, centers not so much on its statistical incidence as an activity as it does on the social recognition and protection of it as an individual, personal prerogative.

The claim of a catastrophic right to a particular therapy should make unjustifiable, with respect to that therapy and that patient, the exercise of a paternalistic therapeutic authority. We might formulate this aspect of the right thusly:

A catastrophically ill patient has the right to be free from any *paternalistic* interference in electing, in consultation with his physician, any therapy whatsoever that does not cause direct harm to others.

This very conservative formulation covers, as a base point, those instances in which only the catastrophic patient is active in the acquisition and administration of the treatment. For instance, herbal remedies – which can be obtained and used without any help from physicians, government, or pharmaceutical companies – are being tried by many PWAs. Society would want to intercede (most appropriately in the person of the patient's physician), at least in an initial instance of what appeared to be the precipitous or uninformed selection of a therapy that struck us as equivalent to suicide; if the catastrophic patient persisted in such a choice, however, we would have to accede as certainly as we would have to accede to the firm determination of a person who *refused* treatment on religious, conscientious, or medical grounds.

The point to be taken here is that, insofar as the consequences of the election of a catastrophic treatment fall narrowly on the patients themselves, their right to elect such a treatment is practically absolute. I add the consultative proviso to cover the obligation of society to protect everyone affected from the unintended and unwanted consequences of acting in ignorance, but the consultative role of the physician – whose active participation is neither needed nor sought in the acquisition and administration of the treatment – is just that and no more. Society ought not to claim a veto in the determination of completely self-acquired and self-administered catastrophic therapies. Thus, the qualification that the limiting condition for this right involves the production of direct rather than indirect harm. Obviously, to the extent that no person is an island, their health or survival is bound to produce some social ripples – and those ripples will touch the public health interests we considered earlier in the context of general and ordinary policy. However, if we recognize a catastrophic right of symmetrical force and limits with the right to refuse treatment, then the actions of the patient which fall completely within his own competence and resources should not be interfered with.

An extension of this principle would include all of those catastrophic therapies which *did* necessitate the active participation of a physician, so long as the professional judgment and ethics of the cooperating physician permitted. In such a case the exercise of a catastrophic right is conditional upon the catastrophic patient enlisting a professional ally who is a member, in good standing, of the therapeutic system. Such a limited paternalistic condition is subject to attack from two quarters. Some argue that it is too restrictive of the exercise of catastrophic rights, and urge that physicians ought to regard themselves as morally bound to place the deliberate choices of their catastrophic patients above their professional judgment. Others argue that it is too liberal a conception of catastrophic rights, and that it will open the way to exploitation of catastrophic patients by unscrupulous "snake-oil" doctors. I believe that both of these objections are ill-considered.

In the case of the supposed moral obligation – some enthusiasts go so far as to claim a legal obligation – of physicians to be unconditionally governed by their catastrophically ill clients, there is, I believe, a confusion concerning what is entailed in the engagement of professional services. Architects are supposed to build the sort of house we want just as lawyers are supposed to plead our case according to our directions, but these desires and directions of the client cannot and should not hold boundless sway over a genuine professional. Architects must conform to the building code, and may even refuse to continue to practice for a client who demands the erection of an aesthetic monstrosity. Similarly, a lawyer can, and should, excuse himself from the service of a client who seeks to direct him in ways which would implicate him in an unlawful undertaking, or which would otherwise compromise his professional ethics. To put it baldly: a professional is not simply a person in the business of rendering a service for fee; he is in the business of rendering a particular and special sort of service – one bound by an authoritative system of values and standards – which is to say, a professional one. The customer of a professional service can never "always be right," and when doing business conflicts with being a professional, being a professional should come first.

Something of the same misunderstanding of professionalism is present in the objections of those who argue that the precedence of catastrophic rights over the exercise of paternalistic authority will result in the emergence of a class of opportunistic AIDS doctors. Professional bodies in the West are governed by a special tribunal of colleagues who are usually vested with sufficient authority by government to enable them to effectively regulate their membership in accordance with specific standards of professional conduct. Malpracticing physicians are subject to censure or even expulsion by their respective professional associations, and we can look to this fact of the professional's life to act as a bulwark against abuses of their catastrophic patients.

It is important, in this connection, to underscore a feature of the situation of the catastrophic patient that has little to do with the usual considerations brought to the calculation of medical utilities. The implacable character of AIDS – and several other catastrophic illnesses – as it contrives to systematically undermine the spirits as well as the bodies of PWAs, threatens to impose upon them the horrible passivity of a "victim." *Acting* in the face of that threat can become an imperative for many who recognize, in the intellectual and practical effort to fight back, one of the essential keys to the maintenance of their continued will to hope and live. Thus, when we turn from the special perspective of the catastrophic patient, to our consideration of the erosion of the ability of the sick to bring their ordinary powers to the task of directing their treatment, it is clear that we must adjust our sense of the importance of being protected from medical opportunists and quacks. There are real and substantial dangers to health from these quarters, to be sure, but, as Kevin Brown of the Vancouver PWA Society was fond of wryly putting it, "Let me tell you about dangers to health!" It is always easy, from the comparatively Olympian perspective of good health, to point out after the fact that a gamble on the part of the catastrophically ill didn't pay off. For their part, they stress that they live, act, and speak from Another Kingdom, and their choices should always have the fundamental fact of their altered condition as the most relevant background consideration.

A catastrophic illness changes a lot of things for those who suffer from it, and one of the things most changed – at least for those with the strength to use it – is the importance of the personal freedom to seek treatment. A migraine sufferer faces a lifetime of headaches, and has a personal interest in participating in a social effort that stands a reasonable chance of improving their life in the future. Whatever else going along with the social plan has to recommend it in this connection, it can at least be fairly claimed that it can't kill you. But PWAs can have a very limited future, and their individual interest may best be served by resisting social limitation of their freedom to try to save themselves. As pointed out earlier, they are falling into an abyss, and it would be irrational for them to deny themselves the possibility of climbing out of their dilemma in order that their ordinary interests as consumers of ropes could be served.

An example of paternalistic management of the catastrophically ill will help establish my point. PWAs are, quite naturally and wisely, always on the look-out for substances which could possibly enhance their faltering immune systems. Among the substances that have been widely tried in Canada is dextran sulphate – a heart medicine which has been used in Japan, with very little incidence of reported toxicity, for over twenty years. Quite apart from whatever claims might be made for (or against) its efficacy – which are, from the point of view of the issue at hand, not strictly relevant – it represented a relatively innocuous opportunity for individual experimentation by PWAs.

However, the regulatory authorities at Canada's Health Protection Branch (HPB) routinely refused to approve its prescription by physicians for this purpose, making it necessary for buying clubs and resourceful individual PWAs to import it from Bermuda. Ironically, there are huge supplies of dextran sulphate in Ontario, and a CBC TV *Journal* report on the controversy surrounding the drug showed barrels of the stuff piled up in a warehouse only miles away from many of its consumers in Toronto, who were on the phone to a bemused pharmaceutical wholesaler in Nassau.

There was a way out of this madness, available in a special set of HPB regulations called the "Emergency Treatment Provisions." The Emergency Treatment Provisions were not enacted with such a use in mind. Rather, they were put in place to deal with special instances of the need for an established therapy, on an individual patient basis, when the therapy was not licensed for sale in Canada. There are, for instance, parasitic infections endemic to the tropics which are rarely or never seen in Canada, and for which no drug company could expect to find an established Canadian market. As a result, the companies who sell medicines for these infections never bother to seek approval here. Rather than deprive patients of such an "orphan drug," the HPB can use the emergency treatment provisions to deal efficiently with the specific and special treatment dilemma posed by a tropical disease.

Notwithstanding this historical account of their origins, the emergency treatment provisions authorize the officials of the HPB to circumvent a significant portion of their own regulations, depending on their judgment of the merits of the case made out to them. As such, the provisions form a legal loophole through the ordinary obstacles of the regulatory apparatus, and it is natural that they should be energetically applied to by catastrophic patients and their physicians. Indeed, and in specific response to these very requests (along with the political pressure created by AIDS people behind them), the HPB had instituted a special program called, appropriately, the Emergency Drug Release Program (EDRP).

Now for the point of the story. Dextran sulphate was, at the time of the *Journal* report in April 1989, specifically advertised by the HPB in their February publication of *Issues* as an EDRP drug available to physicians caring for PWAs. One would think that any issue of a misplaced or inappropriate paternalism had been thoroughly – indeed institutionally – addressed.

But not so. Alistair Clayton, the head of the Federal AIDS Centre, and the chief where the Canadian governance of AIDS and its therapies is concerned, spoke on camera of dextran sulphate as though he were discussing the importation of wildly pornographic magazines rather than a type of medicine. Evidently very uncomfortable, and speaking as though the production of sound was accomplished only by overcoming the operation of powerful natural forces within him, he identified caution and control as the very essence of public health wisdom. Finally, in a ghastly effort to appear game, he asked the interviewer if *she* could guarantee that dextran sulphate was completely safe for use by PWAs. While viewers reeled under the impact of this *non sequitur*, other officials of the HPB appeared on our screens to cheerfully advise that there would be absolutely no difficulty with the compassionate release of dextran sulphate if it were requested by a physician who judged it could be useful in the treatment of a catastrophically ill patient under his care. Yes *and* no, or "P and not-P" as it appears in the introductory logic texts. It was, appropriately enough, the perfect situation in which to apply the empirical method of science and establish the truth with an experiment.

And so it came to be, with the pitiless cameras soaking it all up, that the nation watched as the Health Protection Branch was telephoned by a charmingly skeptical AIDS doctor. Although, as he explained to the interviewer, he had long since abandoned the possibility of eliciting cooperation from the Branch, he good-naturedly grasped the levers of the bureaucracy in a final and (unknown to the official with whom he conferred) extremely public effort to get the HPB to release some dextran sulphate for the use of his patient. And the answer was, of course ... "forget it!" It was the sort of moment that earns an institution of government an immediate installment of its Warholian allotment of fame. And it was even mildly comic – as long as you saw it as just another version of Jack Nicholson trying to get a sandwich the way he wanted it in *Five Easy Pieces*.

More seriously, it gave dramatic force to the idea that it is a cruel sort of authoritarian dumbness to paternalistically interfere with the freedom of the catastrophically ill, aided by their physicians, to make their own assessment of the risks they run in using an untested drug, and to take their own chances. It is, after all, they who are dying, and who must bear the consequences of their mistakes.

There will certainly be mistakes made, but it is important to recognize that where catastrophic illness is concerned, virtually all treatments are more likely than not to be *some* form of mistake – even those proposed by the most circumspect medical professionals. The central issue can never be about being sure or making mistakes in an area where – by definition – nobody really knows what to do. The issue is, rather, who has the ultimate right to control the course of therapy and make those inevitable mistakes?

In the wake of the *Journal* broadcast, the HPB hastily announced that there had been some unaccountable error made in response to the physician's request. That obstacle had been cleared away, they said, and, moreover, the policy was now to be that virtually all requests for the release of drugs on compassionate grounds would be cooperatively and speedily processed. Behind the scenes at the Branch, at least one high official was removed (a man who once wistfully observed to me during an interlude in a meeting that he wished that the B.C. Civil Liberties Association would sue the HPB for the rights of AIDS patients. "Then we could all go to court and have polite intellectual fun for years and years. Just like the Americans do it.") Reflecting on the radical about-face on dextran sulphate, the *Globe and Mail*, editorially commented (on March 1) that while "few would argue with the principle of catastrophic rights" (a kind plug for my thesis by the editors who had conferred with me earlier), the new policy seemed rather precipitous. The editorial concluded by posing the global question: ". . . is the policy of untested drug approval fundamentally wise?" The answer to which is, at least and in part: as far as *paternalistic* interference with the therapeutic autonomy of the catastrophically ill goes, it most certainly is.

While delighted by the avowed commitment of the Branch to the immediate liberalization of its administration of the Emergency Drug Release Program, experienced observers remained wary. The Branch reacted quickly to the enormous public and political pressure facing it in the wake of the televised attention given its whimsical and *ex cathedra* administrative style. But religious conversions that hatch under the TV lights are notoriously mutable, and no one whose interests are intimately affected is likely to forget that a regulatory conversion that had its inspiration in a few feet of videotape may not outlast the ordinary range of public memory. Besides, there are, as we have already seen, more reasons for the social control of therapy than paternalistic ones.

*Conservation
of limited
health-care
resources
revisited*

As IN THE case of the ordinary arguments in support of medical paternalism, catastrophic illness presents us with exceptional and excepting circumstances when we turn to the issue of cost-effectiveness. It is clear that governing the administration of therapies – "You may take this medicine; you may not take that" – is positively related to the conservation of health-care resources in the case of the non-catastrophically ill. The sooner we make this class of patients well, the sooner they will no longer be drawing on our resources to care for them. But the catastrophically ill are dying, and dying because medical science is powerless to save them. The only reasonable claim that can be made for the governance of their individual therapies is that such a restriction of their freedom may prevent them from dying sooner as the consequence of an unsuccessful gamble on an unproven treatment. As for the cost of attending to the special palliative crises associated with dying itself, such expenses form a constant element of the catastrophic situation – we can pay them now or pay them later.

Thus, to the extent that we believe in science, we must suppose that the net effect of catastrophic rights will generally be to shorten the lives of those who exercise them, and thus proportionally spare the health-care resources that would have been needed by such patients had they chosen to be governed by the therapeutic authorities. From the point of view of medical science, the exercise of a catastrophic right to an unapproved drug is tantamount to refusing to follow doctor's orders. Refusing the best medical advice in the face of a catastrophic prognosis must be expected, on the average, to hasten death. This claim may startle some readers, especially those who see the point of catastrophic rights in terms of saving lives. It is true that catastrophic rights will be exercised, wherever they are recognized, in the hope of preserving life. It is also true that they will, at least sometimes, have precisely that effect. If, for instance, aerosolized pentamidine had been made more widely available earlier, as a majority of PWA advocacy groups urged, many lives could have been spared. But there is a difference between the special instance and the general run of the cards. The general run of medical probabilities and actualities conclusively favours science, and personal gambles that fly in the face of general truth will generally lose. The question then is, who should have the final say about where the chips are put down when the medical situation is catastrophic? My contention is that there are rights issues which must be engaged in answering that question which supersede the narrow matter of what, from moment to moment, the experts advise. However, the house always wins, and players who choose not to accept that reality as the dominant consideration governing their play will *in general* be out of the game sooner rather than later.

This view of medical economics can be attacked from another perspective, however, when we turn to the consideration of the claim that the governance of access to experimental drugs is fundamental to the protection of our ability to achieve scientific and medical progress, and that such progress directly affects the costs of caring for the future patients that we must anticipate facing over the next decades or generations. We may chalk up a net health-care saving on those catastrophically ill patients who vigorously exercise their catastrophic rights now, but this small saving could be more than offset by the fact that in losing them to scientific experimentation, we have – arguably – lost a large portion of our opportunity to find a cure for their disease. This may be seen as a very expensive loss when we reflect that many more persons can be expected to get AIDS, and their care will command a very substantial portion of our health-care resources. On this account, we must attend to the issue of the maintenance of subject discipline as an integral and important element of a far-seeing calculation of health-care responsibilities and expenditures.

Before we turn to doing so, we should notice that something interesting has happened. The case against recognition of catastrophic rights has usually been pressed as an amalgamation of paternalistic, economic, and scientific concerns. "They will kill themselves in droves, or they will royally mess up their already delicate health – leaving us to expensively tend to the shattered remains, and while they're at it they will make it impossible for us to make scientific headway." The first two elements of this case cannot withstand close scrutiny if catastrophic rights are given even a conservative force. Thus, it turns out that the full burden of supporting the argument against catastrophic rights must shift to the shoulders of what is ordinarily thought of as only a single element in a set of countervailing considerations. In returning to the issues surrounding human experimentation on catastrophic drugs, we are coming to the heart of the theoretical part of our problem.

VI.
Science
and Rights

NOBODY is claiming that the acquisition of scientific knowledge, *per se*, is the public interest which is thrown into the balance against the exercise of catastrophic rights. We don't limit individual rights and freedoms – in North America at least – in order to gain knowledge for its own sake. It is not "pure," but rather "applied" or "mandated" science that is at issue – scientific research as an instrumental good.

Having set aside paternalism and the *direct* economic benefits to be gained through the restriction of the therapeutic autonomy of the catastrophically ill, two public health interests remain which depend upon the achievement of scientific progress. The first of these is, as indicated above, the economic savings to be realized indirectly, or over the long term. The discovery of a cure or vaccine or more effective treatment that may be achieved by limiting the therapeutic freedom of the present generation of patients, would possibly spare us the expense of ineffectively (i.e. expensively) treating all of the future sufferers from such a disease.

The second public interest refers back to "the protection of people," and focuses on the special public health interests engaged when a disease – catastrophic or otherwise – is infectious. When such is the case, a far-seeing governance must consider not only the economic consequences of compromising our ability to make scientific progress, but also the more direct costs to its citizens in the continued human suffering which such medical progress could end.

Both of these public interests are substantial, and the latter is, in my view, vital. (Although in the case of AIDS, the fact that the disease is an STD rather than contagious is of central importance, as per our discussion of this point earlier.) But recognizing that does not settle the question of how we ought to range catastrophic rights against the public health interests linked to the maintenance of scientific progress. Rather, it helps us refine the issue before us, and focuses our attention on two questions that are often begged in arguments that pit the needs of science against the therapeutic autonomy of individuals. These two questions are: what can science really do? and how can it do it?

There is, first of all, the issue of what science can reasonably hope (and hence promise) to attain if it is given its way. In this connection, it is important to recall something that became apparent when we considered the limits placed upon the right to refuse established medical treatment. When a vital and *attainable* public interest – such as the extirpation of a disease in the context of a program of vaccination – was in the balance, the individual right to refuse was set aside. I emphasize the attainable character of the public interest in such cases, since it is often overlooked that it is as important a feature of the public interest argument as is the vital character of the interest protected. When we are imposing a substantial limitation upon the rights of real people, we ought to have the actual attainment of a vital public interest to put in the balance.

Consider, in this connection, what our response would be to the claims of a "College of Philippine Faith-healers" to be able to provide us with vital public health interests such as the extirpation of the cancers. We would not limit the therapeutic autonomy of cancer patients in order to make the "research" of such faith-healers possible – not because the public health interest in vanquishing cancer isn't vital, but simply because we do not, as a society, have faith in the ability of faith-healers to deliver it.

So the question of what science can actually do if it is given its way, in the specific context of the catastrophic illnesses, should be examined rather than taken for granted. It is important to recognize that there are really two claims made in this connection by medical science. The first is stated forcefully, confidently, and often: "if we are *not* given a range of therapeutic authority with which to limit the freedom of experimental subjects, we will *never* be able to do genuinely scientific work." The second is stated less forcefully, more diffidently, or never: "if we *are* given the authority we demand, we will deliver the sought-after public health interests in the form of safer, more effective, and more economical treatment *soon*." The second claim is often taken to be a corollary of the first – which it most definitely is not – but it is this claim of a positive therapeutic competence which is, of course, the real justification for the granting of a range of authority over the freedom of individuals. Real rights shouldn't be limited on the strength of a mere logical possibility of their being justified by some off-setting vital public good.

I do not propose to attack medical science's record of contribution to human welfare. But a realistic measure of modesty is called for, which is conspicuously absent from most of the responses of the medical establishment when the rights of the catastrophically ill are at issue. In this connection, it is relevant to consider the account of medical experimentation offered by Lewis Thomas in his book *The Youngest Science*. Hardly a maverick, Dr. Thomas was president of the famed Memorial Sloan-Kettering Cancer Center in New York City, and is now its chancellor. Speaking of work on the endorphins, he says:

> Making guesses at what might lie ahead, when the new facts have arrived, is the workaday business of science, but it is never the precise, surefooted enterprise that it sometimes claims credit for being. Accurate prediction is the accepted measure of successful research, the ultimate reward for the investigator, and also for his sponsors. Convention has it that prediction comes in two sequential epiphanies: first, the scientist predicts that his experiment will turn out the way he predicts; and then, the work done, he predicts what the experiment says about future experiments, his or someone else's. It has the sound of an intellectually flawless acrobatic act. The mind stands still for a moment, leaps out into midair at precisely the millisecond when a trapeze from the other side is

hanging at the extremity of its arc, zips down, out, and up again, lets go and flies into a triple somersault, then catches a second trapeze timed for that moment and floats to a platform amid deafening applause. There is no margin for error. Success depends not so much on the eye or the grasp, certainly not on the imagination, only on the predictable certainty of the bars to be caught. Clockwork.

It doesn't actually work that way; and if scientists thought it did, nothing would get done; there would be only a mound of bone-shattered scholars being carried out on stretchers.

In real life, research is dependent on the human capacity for making predictions that are wrong, and on the even more human gift for bouncing back to try again. This is the way the work goes. The predictions, especially the really important ones that turn out, from time to time, to be correct, are pure guesses. Error is the mode.

We all know this in our bones, whether engaged in science or in the ordinary business of life. More often than not, our firmest predictions are chancy, based on what we imagine to be proba-bility rather than certainty, and we become used to blundering very early in life ...

Pg. 81-2 *The Youngest Science.*
New York: The Viking Press, 1983

And, just in case this conjures up that other, and more subtle, dithyrambic vision of science – proceeding in an orderly progress from negative result to negative result, ruling out the dead ends as it relentlessly homes in on truth and success, Lewis Thomas reminds us of the story of the discovery of the cure for pernicious anemia in 1926. Thomas sets it up by recounting the "bare out-line" of the story, which appears to "illustrate the neatness and precision with which biomedical research can sometimes solve major disease problems." Learning from a publication of Dr. William Whipple that dogs that had been made anemic by repeated bleedings were helped by being fed large quantities of fresh liver, Dr. George Minot decided to try feeding liver to his pernicious anemia patients. It worked, and we might be tempted to consider it the first scientific observation of vitamin B12 at work in curing pernicious anemia.

But then Thomas drops the clanger, pointing out that this

"bare outline" is actually a cosmetic gloss for a remarkable chain of events, bound together by a kind of serendipitous charm, and culminating in what he describes as "the final piece of luck":

> Looking back at the events, doctors are now generally agreed that Whipple's dogs could have had nothing at all like pernicious anemia. Their anemia was actually due to iron deficiency brought about by repeated haemorrhage, and the response to liver was almost undoubtedly caused by the very large dose of liver used for feeding. It was the wrong model to use for studying pernicious anemia, and it led straight to the Nobel prize.   Pg. 255, *Ibid.*

I do not believe that this is the sort of anecdote that should persuade sensible people, and least of all sensible patients, to abandon science. It is, in fact, the sort of story that a supremely confident scientist can afford to tell on his craft. Rather than invite general skepticism about the power of research, it should probably bring to mind the old proverb from sports, which is that "the good player is always lucky." Nonetheless, it reminds us of something that is often overlooked, and which is relevant when considering the conflict between catastrophic rights and the claims of science: it is reasonable to have faith in science, but unreasonable to expect that it can produce a cure for the cancers, or for Alzheimer's, or the common cold, or AIDS in a couple of years – or perhaps even in the next generation.

Guessing what science can do about AIDS if it is given its way is, to say the least, difficult. At the Montreal Conference, Jonas Salk made a very big splash with his claim that there was definitely "light at the end of the tunnel" (I thought this a strange metaphor to be chosen by anyone who had lived through the Johnson administration's luckless use of it when pronouncing on the progress of the war in Viet Nam), but most investigators and PWAs were discouraged by the very slow pace of progress. For PWAs in particular, the situation could be summed up in a phrase: "Nothing yet and nothing much soon."

So what can PWAs and society realistically hope for from medical research in the near to medium term? Having pointed out the obvious, which is that we all pray for a cure and vaccine in the next couple of months, realism would suggest that progress will go forward on something like the model afforded us by the cancers. Here we have a family of illnesses and outcomes which bears at least a rough resemblance to the medical picture painted by AIDS. If we accept this analogy, we must accept the likelihood that progress, when it comes, will most likely be incremental rather than decisive (which in fact has been the case so far in the fight against the opportunistic infections with which AIDS kills), and that experimentation will have a role to play in making the disease yield its ground in inches. This is a good thing, a great thing really, but it has two unhappy implications that must be faced.

First of all, if the progress on AIDS that is attainable by medical science is anything like the progress we have experienced with the cancers, it will most definitely *not* produce health-care savings. Indeed, we can expect it to produce health-care costs which we would have been spared in its absence. We have noted that one of the most common arguments for sacrificing individual rights to those public interests connected with the claims of science rests with the economic consideration that if we do so we will be able to offer more safe and effective treatments to future patients. But just as this is probably a good bet, it is probably an even better bet that those "better" treatments will not be cheaper treatments, or treatments which spare our limited health-care resources. They will, in all probability, be the most expensive treatments imaginable in the case of a catastrophic illness – the kind that buy time without curing. Of course, an outright cure or vaccine would almost certainly be cheaper, but we should not, given that a "magic bullet" is unlikely to be forthcoming, forget the very unpleasant but centrally relevant fact that next to a patient who is very quickly cured, the cheapest patient to treat is one who is very quickly dead. Treatment of the cancers is now a medical industry in its own right, and consumes a huge portion of our resources for the provision of health care.

Only the most radical Western critics have ventured to suggest that we halt the medical research which has produced this situation (although enthusiasm about the application of the technologies made possible by some of this research is becoming tempered – as per the earlier quoted comments of Callahan of the Hastings Center), but the swelling cost of health care must certainly give pause to anyone urging that we ought to let science have its way – to the detriment of individual rights – so that we can save money! One of the comments that can be made with most confidence about the strengths and weaknesses of modern medical science is that – with but few extraordinary exceptions – they are perfectly balanced to generate remarkably expensive standards of treatment for serious illnesses in general, and catastrophic illnesses in particular.

Of course, against all of this it can be argued that no matter how long or expensive or uncertain the outcome of the journey, science is our best chance of eventually finding an effective cure for the cancers and AIDS and other catastrophic illnesses, and that such cures represent a great social good. This is a truth that is at once irresistible and deeply troubling. It is irresistible because it is simply reasonable to recognize science – even with its very considerable limitations clearly in view – as the most productive mode of engaging the material world that we have ever possessed as a species, and it is simply human to acknowledge the gift of life as a good. It is troubling, however, because the "no matter how long or expensive or uncertain the outcome" phrase is becoming painfully real for us in the form of a seemingly open-ended range of health-care expenses, and we must wonder if we have confounded the provision of health-care with a necessarily losing battle against mortality which is compromising our ability to provide other badly needed social services. However, and to bring this discussion back to the matter at hand, even if we decided, as a matter of policy, to beggar our treasuries in order to pursue such an ephemeral public health goal as immortality, that wouldn't automatically make it *just* to limit the individual rights and liberties of our citizens for it into the bargain.

Which brings us to the second unhappy implication of the incremental character of the growth of scientific knowledge and the medical progress which is dependent upon it; it is cold comfort for just about everybody who is HIV infected now. For while we are talking about the hope of medical progress, they are living with, and for, the hope of escaping their personal catastrophe. That hope is intimately linked to their ability to get access to those few drugs which are judged to show some promise as therapies for AIDS. When we deny any part of that access on the strength of a calculated guess that it may make it possible for us to achieve a public interest somewhere down the road, we do them a certain and substantial harm now. There is a disanalogy here with those instances in which the right to refuse medical treatment was limited by the presence of a public health interest. For, in each of those instances, we noted that the public interest was not only clear and vital, but *realistically and presently attainable* – as opposed to speculative.

But considerations of the limits of what science can do, while undermining arguments against catastrophic rights which depend upon the public interest of conserving our health-care resources, do not operate very powerfully in reverse as a support for catastrophic rights in a North American medical environment. If forced participation, as a subject in medical experimentation, were a feature of our politics, the limitations of science would be among the most powerful elements of a civil rights case against the practice. Such a case would, in fact, be much the same as the established one made for the right to refuse medical treatment. But as it is, the only patients who participate in any medical experimentation in the United States or Canada are those who are personally convinced that there is a possible benefit to either themselves or to society in doing so; that is, they share the very general faith in the ability of science to produce results. Whatever their case for special access, it can hardly make sense for them to demand adjustments in how the enterprise goes forward – especially if those are adjustments which tend to weaken the enterprise – on the strength of an argument that science isn't really all that powerful anyway! That would be as foolish as a group of citizens demanding access to the gold of Fort Knox on the grounds that it really isn't worth very much.

PWAs are not, as a group, about to take any comfort in reflections on the limitations of science, nor do any of them – in North

America – have any need of a special argument for a right to be left alone by science. Far from that being the case, perhaps the fundamental concern of PWAs in this regard is that of being abandoned by a scientific effort which they see as underfunded and misdirected. They want more science rather than less science, and they want that science to be about them and their disease. Such science might well be very expensive – and the treatments discovered by it might be more expensive still – but there is an important distinction between AIDS and such costly beneficiaries of medical progress as the cancers and heart disease which is an important consideration offsetting that expenditure: PWAs are characteristically so young that there can be no danger of confusing their medical salvation with the heedless pursuit of immortality. Indeed, many PWAs have come to the view that society has very discriminating powers of perception when it comes to the extraordinary expense of medical progress, and that their disease seems to be regarded as not worth the cost of the sort of earnest effort that could be expected if the young dying people happened not to be either generally despised or discounted.

Besides, and perhaps even more importantly, AIDS is infectious; it could still engulf a very large proportion of our population. Until this disease has its stinger pulled, we must all live under the apprehension that it can break out of its present limited epidemiological situation and turn into a disaster of World War dimensions. More than any other consideration, it is the infectiousness of AIDS which puts the "vital" in its status as a vital public health concern.

So even though society has no public interest claims that justify overriding catastrophic rights for paternalistic or economic reasons, it still has a case for doing so that is rooted in the most fundamental of public-health concerns – the control of infectious, deadly disease. A fair statement of society's case for exercising a therapeutic authority which limits catastrophic rights would then, at this point in our discussion, go something like this: "Let's say that we give you the ground we previously claimed for paternalistic or economic reasons. That gives a certain real force and range to your idea of catastrophic rights, but still leaves us occupying some territory that we cannot responsibly surrender to you. We cannot abandon our efforts to make scientific headway against your disease, because we have an obligation to protect the health of all of society from infection with it, and we have a related obligation to make such progress for the sake of the very many of our members who may not have your disease now, but who will certainly get it and suffer your fate if we cannot discover a cure or more effective treatments. We have, in a manner of speaking, a 'practice' that extends beyond you to those who remain well now, and those who will fall ill in the future. Thus, your voluntary participation (which is also your vote of confidence in medical science) in our experimental trials of therapies for your illness must continue to be governed by us so as to protect our ability to do science, since we must be governed by our obligation to provide for a broad range of vital public health interests."

This brings us, in my view, to the heart of the public interest argument for limiting the therapeutic autonomy of the catastrophically ill, and it is a strong argument. Strong does not, however, mean absolute. It means, rather, that while there is a compelling public interest case for limiting catastrophic rights, it can only justify limitations of such rights that will materially advance the achievement of the specific and vital public health goal of protecting the ability of medical science to find an effective cure or treatment for AIDS. Only that public purpose is sufficiently compelling, and attainable – at least in the eyes of everyone affected – to prevail against the claim of an individual catastrophic right.

It is important to remember, in this connection, that although individual interests must ordinarily give way to public interests, individual rights ordinarily should not. One properly speaks of individual *interests* being balanced against competing public interests, but individual *rights* are not balanced against public interests – they override them. This refers to the trumping character of rights, which was discussed earlier. However, when we identify a public interest as vital and compelling, the trumping force of competing individual rights is removed, although the situation is then not as simple as one of public interest holding sway over private interest.

An example may help. The first amendment of the U.S. Constitution, and the second section of the Canadian Charter of Rights and Freedoms, identify the intellectual freedoms of thought and speech as the bedrock individual rights of democracy. We will recognize this individual right even when its exercise directly conflicts with an important public interest such as the maintenance of loyal respect for our form of government. The lesson of the McCarthy era in the U.S. – or what the great American journalist, I. F. Stone, called the "haunted Fifties" – was that even the expression of Marxist convictions that our governments should be smashed, and their officials liquidated, must not be prohibited or limited by law. Imagine, however, a pamphlet of Marxist propaganda which contained plans which would make it possible for anyone with fifty dollars and a few simple tools to make a crude atomic bomb. We would certainly, and correctly, prohibit the publication of such a pamphlet as representing an extraordinary threat to a set of public interests properly described as vital. We can argue with the Marxists about how we should, or should not, organize our political lives, but nothing can save us from wholesale slaughter if the power to destroy entire cities is brought within the independent means of anybody and everybody. The logic of the situation is then, in a manner of speaking, that society itself faces a catastrophic situation, and its corporate catastrophic right to protect the conditions for its survival overrides the ordinarily trumping force of individual rights. Such a vital public interest would not legitimize, however, the prohibition of all Marxist propaganda; it could only justify the censorship of Marxist propaganda that contained the cheap bomb plans.

My point here is that an individual right continues to have significance even when its trumping force is overridden by a public interest that is vital and compelling. An overridden right does not subside into the status of a mere interest. It continues to exert its special form of pressure on the case for the existence of the compelling – and hence offsetting – public interest which has, for the moment, dominated. This pressure has several consequences for policy.

Firstly, the right should be overridden only so far as is necessary in order to address the vital and compelling character of the competing public interest. Ordinary public interests do not avail against the expression of a genuine individual right, so if a *proportional* approach to the provision of the vital public interest is possible, it should be vigorously explored. In practical terms, this simply means that the state should always try to find a way around the limitation of an individual right; if it can't avoid the limitation, it should cut into the right only so far as is absolutely necessary.

Secondly, the right is being overridden in order to provide for a specific vital public interest, and hence its limitation must be specific rather than general. A case for the limitation of catastrophic rights which rests upon the vital public interest in finding a cure for AIDS cannot serve as an umbrella under which the therapeutic authorities can limit catastrophic rights for some other reasons – such as paternalistic or economic ones.

Finally, the claim that a public interest exists which is so vital and compelling as to legitimize the setting aside of an individual right places real obligations upon the state with respect to both policy and *performance*. A public interest retains its status as vital or compelling – and hence continues to outweigh individual rights claims – just so long as government's regard for it as such is borne out by the efforts actually made to attain it. There is, of course, no cut and dried way of determining whether or not government is exerting itself in such a way as to sustain the claim that it is pursuing an interest it regards as vital. Nonetheless, it makes sense to accept the principle that, just as there is a difference between interests that are vital, as opposed to those that are merely "nice to have," there is a discernible difference in the behaviour of rational individuals and governments as they seek to provide for one or the other.

These considerations bring us back to one of the questions posed earlier in this chapter: how can science do what it does? In answer to this question, I will first advance a very general policy consideration, and then offer a couple of specific suggestions.

Any public health policy – whether it be a regimen of testing persons in order to identify the infectious, or the imposition of experimental subject discipline by the therapeutic authorities – must finally justify itself at the bar of public health results. Thus, even if general or focused programs of widespread testing looked good in some heaven of intelligence, practical and common sense revealed that in the case of this specific infectious disease they would produce a clear public health disadvantage. Widespread mandatory testing would have done this by undermining one of the key elements of a successful public health fight against AIDS – a relationship of cooperative trust between those who have or are likely to have AIDS and public health workers. Without that relationship, which has, to a remarkable extent, been created and maintained throughout the West, it is unlikely that we would have enjoyed so much success in substantially slowing the spread of the disease among gays, or enjoyed even the limited successes we have had with IV drug abusers.

PWAs are absolutely distinctive as a group of patients because of their social and political cohesiveness. This trait can work against us and damage our scientific efforts to fight AIDS, or it can be made to work for all of us by engaging it in our scientific work much as we have succeeded in engaging it in the cooperative work of public education. As we have seen, after we set aside paternalism and economic concerns as justifications for limiting the therapeutic autonomy of PWAs, what we are really left with, as the specific and vital public interest case, is the attempt to prevent the survival and spread of the disease by finding a cure or more effective treatments for it. **This is a *public* interest which approaches congruence with the *individual* interests of persons with AIDS.** Thus, as a matter of general policy, we should be able to wield our therapeutic authority so that it both serves the public interests that are gained by science, and gives broad scope to the catastrophic rights of PWAs. Science should be able to do what it does in a cooperative, rather than a combative, relationship with PWAs. There should be no doubt that maneuvering room exists which makes such cooperation possible, and I will briefly discuss two "adjustments" in scientific procedure in order to quickly demonstrate that we are not talking about an empty set of alternatives.

I want to return, in the first instance, to our earlier discussion of the role of controls in scientific experimentation. We recall that controls were particularly important in cases in which we had an imperfect grasp of the natural history of a disease. If we don't know precisely what would have happened if we had done nothing – and done nothing with a group of patients that is both like and contemporaneous with the group upon which we have experimented – then we cannot precisely judge the results of the trial of a therapy. These theoretical considerations are clear enough, but their application to human subjects quickly and obviously runs afoul of rather basic moral considerations when one of the perfectly understood features of an imperfectly understood disease is that it is lethal.

Imagine drug X, which has been in fairly common use for one of the terminal cancers for about three years. Drug X is very toxic, a drastic chemotherapy, which has produced an average increase of "good time" of eight months for those patients who have tried and tolerated it. Drug Y is ready for human trials, and it is hoped to offer improvement on X both in terms of efficacy and safety. We can control the trial of Y in two possible ways: the "perfect" scientific option is to control it with an arm which receives only a placebo, and the "imperfect" scientific option is to control it with an arm which receives the established treatment of X. (For the sake of the example, I will stipulate that those who cannot tolerate X are to be excluded from the trial of Y, since they represent a special set of harder cases to treat than is available in a raw average of patients.) The decision to control the trial of Y with a placebo dooms – as far as we can scientifically know – half of those who are persuaded to enter it to eight months less comfortable and productive life. However, it may be argued, that sacrifice buys and pays for scientific progress which cannot be had at any lesser price.

Such an argument misrepresents the needs of science, and hence lends itself to an immoral form of experimentation. We should, in this connection, recall Whipple's dogs – the ones that led to the discovery of a cure for pernicious anemia. All drugs which are to be used in human trials are first very carefully and exhaustively tested on animals, and those experiments can be, and are always, placebo controlled (as well as genuinely and thoroughly blinded in ways that are practically impossible in human trials). Such animal tests do not, of course, obviate the need for human experimentation, and in some circumstances (such as the testing of drugs for the treatment of anxiety) their principal usefulness is necessarily restricted to determining safety rather than efficacy. But in the case of very many diseases, they so thoroughly set the stage for human trials that it is, as a matter of empirical fact, wrong to assert that control with an already established therapy is not enough control. There is, after all, a very good reason for our decision to try Y in the first place, and that is the very carefully determined levels of efficacy and safety that have been established in its animal trials. Y on humans is not a shot in the dark. We might be pleasantly surprised with the human trials, or disappointed, but it is unlikely that we shall see absolutely unlooked-for results. Given that we know at least enough about the disease for which it is to be tried to predict quick death in untreated individuals, insistence upon placebo-controlled human trials would represent an unbalanced, because unrealistic, insistence upon the requirements of an inexact process in a catastrophic situation.

Since the advent of AZT, placebo-controlled trials of catastrophic therapies for AIDS are medical, moral, and – at least coming to be – political monstrosities. PWAs have made significant headway in convincing the therapeutic authorities that they are unacceptable, but the wonder is that such strenuous educational efforts were ever needed. The truth is that these efforts continue to be needed in order to prevent the imposition of experimental protocols which confront the catastrophically ill with the medical version of the Godfather's line: "I made him an offer he couldn't refuse." When such offers continue to be made, we shouldn't be shocked to discover that while almost nobody refuses the deal, they are unlikely to feel honour-bound to keep it.

Similarly, there is the basic issue of the determination of endpoints in the trial of catastrophic therapies. To put this at its crudest – and hence make it conform to some of the truly terrible realities that the catastrophically ill have had to face – should we end such trials when everyone in the control arm is dead, or should we end it when it is clear that everyone in the experimental arm is getting a lot better? I do not believe that the wisdom of Solomon is needed to pick the latter choice as the one that provides both scientific and moral common sense. There can, of course, be a range of difficulties and disagreement associated with the judgment of what "a lot better" means, but uncertainty about that issue should never be confused with uncertainty about the fundamental moral and scientific issue of determining endpoints which reflect the realization that medical science is to be used as an instrument for human good, rather than an end in itself.

I do not offer these very brief points about controls and endpoints to close the issue of how the needs of science and justice can be reconciled. They are meant, rather, to show that what is being discussed is a range of adjustment of the work of science, and not an unbridgeable gulf between being scientifically and morally responsible. Indeed, in the case of placebo-controlled studies at least, the Food and Drug Administration in the U.S. has made it clear, in the most recent update (October 18, 1988) of its regulatory apparatus for "Investigational New Drugs" (the IND process), that it regards such a practice as unnecessary to satisfy its regulatory requirements:

> With respect to study design, the agency recognizes that there has been some confusion about the role of placebo-controlled studies in patients with a life-threatening disease. FDA believes that a requirement for placebo-controlled studies is not appropriate in those situations where there is known to be an effective therapy, for the stage of disease or condition under investigation, that can

improve survival or prevent irreversible morbidity. For example, in the case of symptomatic AIDS or advanced AIDS-related complex (ARC), where zidovudine is known to improve survival, it would not be appropriate to compare a new drug with placebo. Rather, the new drug should be compared with zidovudine. It would also be possible to compare the new drug plus zidovudine with zidovudine alone but in neither case would it be necessary to deny patients therapy with zidovudine which is known to improve survival. In contrast, where no therapy has been shown to be effective, it is scientifically and ethically appropriate to randomize patients to test drug and placebo. This was done with zidovudine and, by providing early and clear evidence of benefit in terms of improved survival, enabled FDA to confer the rapid approval that made the drug widely available to AIDS patients.

> Department of Health and Human Services, Food and Drug Administration. Investigational New Drug, Antibiotic, and Biological Drug Product Regulations; Procedures for Drugs Intended to Treat Life-threatening and Severely Debilitating Illnesses: 21 CFR Parts 312 and 314 [Docket No. 88N-0359] pg. 19-20

This is progress, but a couple of cautionary notes should temper any celebratory tendencies. First of all, FDA does not make it clear why the confusion is being cleared up in this specific way. It does not say, for instance, that placebo-controlled trials of catastrophic therapies (in circumstances where there exists an established therapy) are positively unethical. It *does* say that it is both "scientifically ethical and appropriate" to control with placebo when nothing has been shown to be effective, and then goes on to take a bow for its role in fast-tracking AZT. None of this carries with it the necessary implication that to test a new AIDS drug with placebo instead of against AZT would be unethical ... only that it would not be appropriate. This can mean several things, and readers are invited to draw whatever implication pleases them most. If you are a particularly tough-minded scientist, you may infer that the FDA regards placebo-controlled trials under such circumstances as more strictly scientific than is practicably attainable – although perfectly ethical – given the political pressure being placed upon its masters in Congress and the Senate. If you are a PWA, you might infer that the lion is at last moving to recline with the lamb, and that the FDA is becoming sensitized to catastrophic rights.

What must be understood, in this connection, is that as important as it is for government to actually move in liberalizing the regulation of catastrophic therapies, it is at least as important for government to tell us *why* it is moving. Indeed, my conviction that this is true has been among the strongest incentives leading me to write about catastrophic rights. There is a world of difference between giving in to political pressure and institutionalizing a principle. The former course of action is the daily life-work of politicians and officials in a pluralistic democracy, and it should never be mistaken for the latter course – which is a much more rare and precious political pearl. Pressuring government to bend a bit is, I suppose, a good thing to do when the cause is just, but such a result is never a lasting one unless the case for justice is made out clearly, *and* publicly accepted by government. Even then, there is a world of difference between government (a) saying what it plans to do and why, and (b) its successfully persuading its officials to actually carry out the plan. This difficulty is compounded when the government's plans involve a therapeutic system over which it has only a limited and oblique measure of control . . . but this is to anticipate the discussion of the regulatory authorities in the next section.

There is yet another practical problem with the FDA placebo-control regulatory policy. The new FDA policy says that when no therapy has been shown to be effective, placebo-controls are the best way to go – and hence the only way acceptable to them. But what counts as "shown to be effective"? If only an experimental trial that is placebo-controlled can count as demonstrating efficacy, then a terrible set of problems ensues. What happens when, for instance, an experimental catastrophic drug has been used extensively in early compassionate therapeutic efforts, and its usefulness and safety have been determined in the rough and tumble of clinical experience? In such a case, an extraordinarily good drug can become established as the therapy of choice long before any organized effort can be or is made to test it in the ordinary way – which is the only way consistent with the FDA approval-track. In such a case, it can be seen by everyone to be immoral to test the drug with a placebo, but if it *isn't* tested with a placebo, the FDA can never pass it (given its present interpretation of its mandate, at least), and the company which developed it can never sell it. One might think that this is such a stupid "catch-22" that it could not possibly hold up the parade for longer than it took to recognize it as a sort of administrative curiosity. To think so would be to err, as we shall see when we consider the scandalous case of ganciclovir and CMV retinitis in the next section.

Realizing all of the moral, legal, political, and economic difficulties that are tangled up with the development of new drugs for catastrophic illness should remind us of our discussion of the limits of what science can do. There are, most definitely and clearly, limits to the power of medical science both to know and to come to know. And these limits constrain not only what medical science is supposed to know, but also all of those areas of human concern and consequence about which it isn't supposed to know – as a scientific discipline – anything whatsoever. There are important matters concerning which it can provide us with no received wisdom, and for which it cannot speak with an authoritative, or even a single, voice. That is not a good reason to give up on science because, simply and starkly, science is the only game in town when medical progress is the prize to be won. It is, however, a good reason for society to recognize that it has very much the same set of responsibilities for the control of its therapeutic authorities as it does for other powerful expert groups whose expertise is not universal – such as, say, the armed forces. We have vested power in these groups which gives them – quite literally, and with no layer of metaphorical fat – the power of life and death over our citizens. What AIDS is doing, among very many other things, is making it apparent that we bear the same civilian responsibility for governing the war against catastrophic disease as we have for governing the other kind of war.

PWAs are, as I have already pointed out, very far from being either medically or scientifically naive. Although there may be individuals among them who are indifferent to the requirements of genuinely scientific research, they are, as a group, naturally committed to making possible the medical progress upon which they pin most of their hopes. The recognition of catastrophic rights by government would not mean that every individual PWA would get everything they want from everyone immediately. But activist PWAs, as a group in North America, are not asking for the moon; they are asking for a measure of respect for their rights as catastrophic patients to be reflected in the way they are treated. That is something that we can respond to as a society, and something that they will respond to as a group. Doing so can close a growing gap between PWAs and society. It is true that the gap tends to hurt PWAs more than "the rest of us" in the short term, but in the long term it is substantially damaging to the most promising and productive elements of our public health fight against AIDS.

We turn now to the question of how all of this theory works back at the real world. In doing so, we need to consider briefly the work of the regulatory agencies of government – the Food and Drug Administration (FDA) in the United States, and the Health Protection Branch (HPB) in Canada. These agencies focus the therapeutic authority of society, and it is important to understand how they try to protect public interests. Then we shall consider some scenarios – situations within which the operation of catastrophic rights are located and defined.

VII.
Therapeutic Anarchy: The FDA and the HPB

ALTHOUGH it may not be as fair to say of government – as it is of philosophy – that it bakes no bread, it is certainly true that the governments of the United States and Canada are not significant productive forces in the development of new drugs. The governance of therapies is, in North America, essentially an effort to direct, steer, and influence a set of forces which have their origins outside of government itself.

Actually, the bureaucracies which regulate drugs in the U.S. (the Food and Drug Administration) and Canada (the Health Protection Branch) are both really just very powerful and complex marketing authorities. Drugs are typically sold rather than given away, and a plenipotentiary marketing authority is, effectively, an absolute authority in terms of its ability to control the medical use of drugs. It may be thought strange to conceive of these powerful agencies of government as just another edition of the "Egg Board," but it is the truth, and a truth that should be as productive of sympathy as disdain for their officials. For while these people are often held responsible for the performance of a large portion of the therapeutic system, they are actually very far from the engine room that moves the drug world along, and they possess almost nothing like a steering wheel or accelerator. What they've got is brakes, and brakes are a clumsy instrument with which to try to impose a refined sort of control over a huge, powerful, and very complex set of productive forces.

I will not pause to consider the deep philosophical implications of all of this. We all know the alternative, and it is an alternative that is in global disarray and retreat. So I will refrain from trotting out my pet "Five Year Plan" for rationalizing and humanizing that part of the productive forces of society that makes medicines ... because I haven't got one and doubt, these days, that I could interest even a Maoist in such an economic antique if I did. Nevertheless, it is important to remember that when we talk about such lofty notions as the "governance of therapies" and "the therapeutic authorities," that nobody at the Egg Board lays eggs.

Still, they govern them, and the FDA and the HPB stand at the very centre of the therapeutic authorities in North America. They are the guardians of the standards which determine whether or not a drug is safe and powerful enough to be offered for sale. The standards used are, simply, the standards of medical science, and hence there is a natural partnership between the scientific community and the drug agencies of government ... although, as we shall see, it is a partnership that has been very badly strained by AIDS.

A comprehensive discussion of the work of the FDA and the HPB is very far beyond the purpose or scope of this essay, and I am not, in any case, expert enough to provide it. In fact, I propose, for the balance of my consideration of them, to simply lump these two very different bodies together as "the regulatory authorities." Before doing so, however, at least one distinguishing characteristic should be pointed out in passing: the very different experiences of the FDA and the HPB with the drug thalidomide, which produced birth defects on a disastrous scale. To make a long story short, the HPB passed it, and the FDA didn't. The thalidomide experience formed a traumatic watershed for the HPB, and has made it extremely wary of the ability of powerful and complex new drugs to reveal toxicity late rather than early – and has also made it painfully conscious of the meaning of "too late" where terrible side-effects are concerned. Interestingly, the opposite experience of the FDA – which very conservatively blocked the general availability of thalidomide in the U.S. – produced exactly the same set of conservative dispositions, although in its case, it is a conservatism tinged with smugness rather than paranoia. If American federal agencies are ever issued with coats of arms, the heraldic banner on the FDA's will read: "We Saved You From Thalidomide." For the Canadians, of course, the banner reads: "Once Burned . . . "

Recalling our earlier discussion of the important public health interests served by the careful determination of safety and efficacy of new drugs, such conservative esprit is probably not such a bad general idea for the regulatory agencies. It is, however, hopelessly at odds with the need for sensitive weighing of cost/benefit ratios in the case of catastrophic therapies, and the related need for flexibility in the special testing standards that are appropriate for their development.

In any case, the regulatory authorities must attempt to impose a public agenda on a clamouring throng of private or personal interests that threaten, in the absence of governance, to generate a therapeutic anarchy. Their efforts, in the case of catastrophic therapies, are attended with special difficulties, as the interests they seek to control are intensified by the very high stakes on the table. In order to understand these difficulties, we need to briefly consider the distinctive relationship the regulatory authorities have with each of the players in the drug development process.

Regulatory
authorities
and the doctors

THE PATIENT needs survival, relief, respite, and hope – and his doctor wants to provide it for him right away. We have attended to the interests of the patient earlier, and considered the impact of a purely patient-driven therapeutic agenda on the public interest. The patient's professional ally has interests as well, and those interests lean heavily in the direction of doing applied as opposed to pure science. And if science in the direct service of a predefined goal – such as helping one's patient survive an otherwise fatal illness – should turn out to be not quite as pure as could be wished for, "well so much the worse for purity!" the activists among the treating doctors chorus. The regulatory authorities are, unsurprisingly, under constant pressure from primary-care physicians to take off the regulative brakes and speed up the introduction of new therapies on both a clinical and experimental basis. When reminded, in the U.S., of the FDA's achievement in blocking the marketing of thalidomide, some of the more outspoken physicians respond that even a broken clock is right at least twice a day, and that the FDA's regulatory gauntlet (which, according to the activists, besides being unresponsive to catastrophic rights, is generally and needlessly inflexible and inefficient) deprives patients of the benefits of far too many promising treatments for us to take intelligent comfort in what it has spared us in the way of harm from drugs.

Besides, as some disgruntled physicians point out, there is a big difference between the intended use of thalidomide – which was the treatment of morning sickness – and the life-saver function of catastrophic therapies. The authorities are, according to this group, constantly misapplying the lesson of thalidomide, which belongs in the regulatory realm of paternalistically protecting people who are suffering from non-catastrophic illnesses.

The primary-care physician of a catastrophically ill person who is a subject in an experimental trial of a new drug is, to wildly understate it, in an interesting professional situation. She is usually in a position to compromise the "blindness" of the subject, being often the first to know about the effects – in her patient at least – of the treatment or placebo. Whatever the formally determined endpoints of the experiment, the primary-care physician may have a different view of the sensible juncture at which to advise her patient to throw in the towel and cease an experimental treatment that is (apparently) either positively harming him or preventing him from trying something else which might provide the help he desperately needs in time.

Regulatory
authorities
and the research group

MEDICAL researchers are not unfeeling brains, disinterestedly and unemotionally searching for a corner of the truth. They are more often than not passionately engaged by the medical implications of their work, and have strongly held views about experimental design that may or may not conform to those of the regulatory authorities. Even before the crisis of regulation that has developed around AIDS, there were rumblings of discontent from researchers about being forced to try to hit constantly moving scientific targets, and about the "inflexible, preconceived criteria concerning study design." Researchers were also growing impatient with the tendency of regulators to focus on "deviations from technical requirements" rather than on whether "despite the deficiencies, the study provides scientific evidence of the drug's effectiveness." (Guidelines from the final report of the Commission on the federal drug approval process. [Washington, D.C.: Government Printing Office, 1982.] As quoted by David Kessler in the *New England Journal of Medicine* in his special article "The Regulation of Investigational Drugs," Feb. 2 1989.)

AIDS has turned up the heat on this debate, and it shouldn't surprise us to learn that it is not only primary-care physicians who end up deciding that their professional and moral obligations cannot be reconciled with the requirements of the regulatory authorities, but medical researchers as well. If the human trials of a promising catastrophic drug will only get regulatory approval if the experiment is to run for three years (a period during which a majority of the subjects would ordinarily be expected to die), an attitude of "agree to anything to get the trial going, and we'll look for fords across the stream before we come to the bridge" can develop.

However informal and necessarily undocumented such attitudes are, they can be transmitted to prospective subjects. If it is difficult to get PWA subjects to feel conscience-stricken about giving priority to their own agenda – as against sticking to the terms of their inclusion in the experiment – *before* they learn of such attitudes, it is impossible afterwards.

Regulatory authorities and the pharmaceutical companies

DRUG COMPANIES are in business to make money. This is not, in our society, a wicked motive, nor is it inconsistent with good corporate citizenship. It is, however, the fact of market life that overshadows all others, and it is well to bear in mind that the North American drug market measures its sales in the billions of dollars. Billions of dollars generate a lot of power, and that power drives medical research directly through the management of the professionals employed by drug companies, and indirectly through the influence it exerts on the flow of funds to granting agencies and academic institutions. Lots of money in search of even more money has a life of its own, if not a mind of its own, and although the agenda of the market is (hopefully) not absolutely inconsistent with the public interest, it would be foolish to look for perfect coincidence.

In the specific case of AIDS, for instance, the industry confronts a business proposition that is clouded with several unattractive uncertainties. First of all, there are the related and fundamental issues of the size of the potential market and the developmental costs of the products. Recent studies of the prevalence of HIV infection indicate that First World incidence of AIDS is being fairly effectively limited to a few specific groups, and it is uncertain that these groups add up to a profitable market for a cure or treatments which could very possibly elude a special research effort costed out in the tens of millions of dollars. There is, to be sure, a huge number of Third World AIDS cases, but the

Third World is a huge market only in terms of its numbers of patients, and most definitely not in terms of the monies with which it could compensate its deliverers.

Furthermore, although there is an enormous First World market for a vaccine, there are fiendishly difficult – i.e. ruinously expensive – research obstacles that stand in the way of such a medical grail. An all out effort to discover an effective and safe vaccine for AIDS has been likened to the effort required to protect humankind from the common cold, but with a much smaller reward for success at the end of the day.

And finally, although treatments for both the viral infections and many of the opportunistic illnesses that characterize full-blown AIDS have very broad general applications and markets, their use for AIDS requires that they be *specifically* tested for safety and effectiveness as therapies for AIDS under the auspices of the regulatory authorities. As the most significant development costs of such drugs are typically incurred satisfying the rigours of the experimental protocols required by the authorities, it just isn't good business to try some drugs for AIDS which might, on purely medical grounds, show some promise. Unsurprisingly, drug companies want a special regulative deal as an incentive to sponsor such drugs for experimental trial as AIDS therapies.

Still, nobody in the industry forgets the huge profits made by Burroughs-Wellcome on AZT – said to be about 60 to 80 million dollars in 1987. Drug development is always a bit of a horse race, with the big prize going to whoever enters the market first with something that works. Even with all of its special uncertainties, AIDS remains a huge business opportunity, with a very big pot of gold at the end of its developmental rainbow, and although drug executives worry that the chance of getting to the reward first simply cannot justify the risk of incurring "out of this business world" developmental costs, they are still in the game. At the Montreal conference, the area set aside for displays was enormous, and it fairly thrummed with a festival atmosphere of commercial bonhomie. Whatever the companies and nations represented were willing to spend on actual drug development and treatment, the display floor presented an evidently irresistible occasion on which to give a high profile to their commitment. The companies giving away free condoms seemed to act as special energizing stations, and rumours of the arrival of yet another car-load of freebies had the effect of transforming even the most staid and conservatively-attired seniors into something like South Sea youths diving for coins thrown from a cruise ship. (One delegate sitting next to me at the airport, waiting for his departing flight, accidentally opened his exquisite leather attache case upside-down, disgorging enough Japanese super-thins and ribbed wonders to last at least a decade of the sexual life of an ordinary mortal. "For my patients," he blushed.) The odd PWAs seen on this floor seemed at once bewildered, exhausted, and appalled at the spectacle of the other side of their story – the side that was about money, careers, and fame for the opportunists and heroes who rush, in about equal measure, to the site of every disaster.

Before indignation becomes our established mood, it is important to recall yet again the fundamental political and economic fact of life at work here, which is the established privatization, in our political system, of the search for new and better medicines. This means that it is the drug companies themselves that always bear the largest share of the costs of searching for safe and effective new therapies. And although they may be – especially recently – subject to a range of pressures and incentives from government to make promising drugs available on a compassionate (i.e. free) basis pending the issuance of a license to actually sell it, they have very little control over the pace of the regulatory process that can either accelerate or retard their ability to earn a return on their investment. This can produce some interesting moral and political dilemmas for drug companies, who sometimes face the unattractive choice of either protesting – which might upset the officialdom that is busy laying their golden egg *and* lead to a public outcry against their gouging selfishness – or keeping quiet and writing off their fiscal beating as part of the cost of doing business in a mixed economy.

Besides, huge business expenses – imposed, in this case, by a combination of the costly character of human experimentation and the related rigours of the regulatory process – can work to the advantage of those who can afford the price of admission. If you have a promising new drug and want to market it, you have to find millions of dollars with which to satisfy the regulatory requirements of government. Only large concentrations of capital can buy the license to play this game, and those who have it are able to use this advantage to buy up the rights to promising drugs relatively cheaply, and prevent the emergence of smaller upstart pharmaceutical companies. Hence, the big companies have a love-hate regard for the high costs of drug development, recognizing that they can either pay a lot of development costs for sure, or maybe pay the market much, much more. Here, as in so many other areas of life, the devil you know (and can profitably live with) is preferable to the other kind.

There are other difficulties that plague the relationship between the pharmaceutical companies and the regulatory authorities. Some of them are produced, ironically, by a heightened ethical consciousness on the part of the regulators that has been created, in large part, by the political effectiveness of PWAs. A case in point is ganciclovir, a drug which has been used successfully – though only experimentally until recently – with AIDS patients infected with the cytomegalovirus (CMV), which can invade the retina of the eye and cause permanent blindness. The Syntex Corporation, which developed ganciclovir, has estimated that 15 to 45 percent of PWAs will eventually develop CMV retinitis. It is also thought the CMV retinitis will become a larger problem as other advances in the treatment of AIDS-related conditions produce longer lifespans for PWAs.

Ganciclovir seems to work in cases of CMV retinitis, and is reportedly successful in stopping (though not reversing) deterioration in the eyesight of those who use it. (This is according to Jerome Groopman of the Harvard Medical School, in his Feb. 13 1989 *New Republic* article, and John S. James in the Dec. 16 1988 *AIDS Treatment News*) Unfortunately, it has a side-effect – the destruction of bone-marrow – which parallels that of AZT, the most important primary treatment for HIV. It is very often the case that patients have had to give up AZT treatment (thus almost certainly shortening their lives) in order to tolerate ganciclovir and, hopefully, enhance the quality of that portion of life remaining to them. This poignant situation has made the search for alternatives to ganciclovir an urgent priority.

Although it established itself in compassionate clinical use with over 5000 patients in the last three years (at a reported cost to Syntex of over 25 million dollars when research and development expenses are counted in), the approval of ganciclovir by the FDA was held up because it had never been tested in a placebo-controlled trial. Recently, but belatedly, it was approved on the basis of a retrospective analysis of the histories of about 50 cases which a Boston physician had documented with photographic records. But this is a story that no one can tell as directly or as knowledgeably as John S. James of *AIDS Treatment News* in an article entitled "Drug Trial Snafu: The Mandate For Ignorance":

> We use the term "mandate for ignorance" to refer to a hidden but, we believe, enormously important problem in the effective management of clinical trials.
>
> It is widely agreed that a placebo trial (or any other drug trial in which patients are assigned at random to two or more treatment possibilities) is unethical unless the researchers can state an honest "null hypothesis" – that is, unless they really do not know which of the treatment arms is better. For example, a placebo trial is unethical *if the researchers know that* the drug works better than no treatment. But if they *do not know*, then the study is OK, and they are free to proceed with it.
>
> This ethical standard is obviously intended to safeguard the welfare of patients who become subjects in experimental trials. The idea is that subjects should not have to risk a placebo unless nobody knows whether the drug or placebo is better. But the ganciclovir history shows that this well-meaning ethical standard also has monstrous consequences, because it puts a premium on ignorance.
>
> Why have drug companies become so adamant about refusing compassionate access to AIDS treatments, access commonly available for cancer and other diseases? One reason is to force patients into placebo trials – trials often so poorly designed and poorly publicized that few would enter them voluntarily. But

another reason is that drug companies must remain ignorant of how well their own products work, lest that knowledge ethically bar them from conducting the very trials which the FDA requires for approval!

This catch-22 is exactly what happened to Syntex with ganciclovir. And it has terrified other companies into denying compassionate use, and thereby refusing to learn how to use their new drugs effectively except as the result of cumbersome, years-long formal trials.

What should Syntex have done with ganciclovir? Everyone seems to agree that the company should have run placebo trials early – in what is being called "the window of opportunity" to conduct clinical trials – before the public or even the researchers know whether the drug works or not. In other words, the trial must be run before compassionate use – lest the knowledge that the drug does work makes it impossible to run the trials. But in practice, trials have usually taken years to set up and conduct. Therefore, compassionate use must be denied for those years.

This mandate for ignorance not only denies compassionate access to patients; it also saps the vitality of the entire clinical-research enterprise. It requires that companies not know that their drug works until after they run formal trials – not before. But companies have little motivation to invest money in trials unless they believe that the drug does work – the same belief that would make those trials unethical. So nothing happens.

One consequence is that drug companies refuse to cooperate when physicians want to test new uses for products in development. Besides other problems such as the fear of liability if things go wrong, the company could lose its window of opportunity if things go right.

Therefore the mandate for ignorance not only destroys the commercial incentive to run trials, it also forbids the normal exploratory phase of science – which here would be physicians trying experimental drugs in compassionate, well-supported attempts to treat patients. As a result, clinical trials must be designed in a vacuum – based on whatever theories are fashionable, rather than on exploratory experience of what actually works in practice. The result is irrelevant, indecisive, and ultimately ineffectual clinical trials, when they happen at all.

In a recent editorial in the *Journal of the American Medical Association*, a former head of the FDA urged a re-examination of "all the assumptions on which the scientific requirements of the

present system (of drug approvals) are based" (November 25, 1988; see also *The New York Times*, Medical Science section, December 6, 1988). We hope that this mandate for ignorance will be one of the issues addressed.   *AIDS Treatment News*
Issue Number 71, December 16 1988

Mr. James' comments remind us of the earlier quoted regulatory rewrite of the FDA in which the condition suggested as ethical for a placebo-controlled trial of a catastrophic drug was that there was no existing drug "shown to be effective," and it reveals the very elastic and slippery nature of the concept of a "null hypothesis." In the case of ganciclovir, it couldn't be tested in order to see if it worked – using the regulatory standards of the FDA – because it worked. But did *everybody* agree that it worked? Obviously, there is an important sense in which the FDA wasn't satisfied that the evidence for that was clear enough to warrant licensing of it for sale. But if the evidence wasn't clear enough for that, why wasn't it *unclear* enough to posit a null hypothesis? And the answer to that question is, of course, that it depended upon who you asked. After all, we are talking about inductive "proof" in science, which is to say that we are talking about probabilities. Even the most stringent tests of the regulatory authorities do not guarantee that the offspring of the users of a new drug aren't going to grow enormous warts instead of ears; they simply establish a very high probability that such side-effects will not occur. So the question of how high the probability of efficacy and safety ought to be in order to show effectiveness is a judgment call. That the FDA should slice the baloney so that ganciclovir couldn't be licensed for sale *because the probability that it worked was so high that it was unethical to test it in a placebo-controlled trial in order to establish the probability at an even higher level* is, besides being an example of nickel-plated nuttiness, a demonstration of how fraught with difficulty is the null hypothesis ethical standard. As one wag put it to me: "Getting and keeping a null hypothesis is as easy as getting and keeping good gas mileage in your car – just lie." Behind this sarcasm, there is more than a grain of truth.

When considering the relationship between the regulatory

authorities and the drug companies, it is well to remember that in a therapeutic system as focused upon medicines as ours, the companies are among the most important *productive* elements at work for us. Whatever conception of catastrophic rights we arrive at must take into account the fact of market life which provides that, if the exercise of such rights becomes a disincentive to the producers of drugs, there may well be fewer drugs developed. As the necessarily anonymous executive of a pharmaceutical company put the case to me: "It's important for you people to remember that when interests are as large as ours, they *become* rights." Beyond giving rise to the reflection that satire has no future, this insistence should give us some sense of the spirit in which some of the companies regard their power. In any case, it is clear that in pressing a claim for catastrophic rights on government, we should be aware that a radical formulation of those rights by government could quite possibly chill some of the market forces that are the source of promising therapies for the catastrophically ill.

I don't think, however, that PWAs or their allies should be so terror-stricken by this threat that they are warned off the process of making sense of and working for catastrophic rights. Market-economy democracies are very familiar with capital's threat that if it can't do business exactly the way it wants to, it won't do business at all. In a sense, the history of "mixing" the mixed economies of the West is the history of standing up to this threat as the forceful expression of yet one more big interest among others. Still, we should never forget the homily that warns us to be mindful of our prayers – just in case they're answered. Any well-considered account of catastrophic rights must bear in mind that powerful market forces are a fundamentally important part of the therapeutic picture.

Besides these three main groups, the regulatory authorities must also confront the claims made on its resources and patience from several others as well. Hosts of expert groups, both within and outside of government, spring up around significant policy issues, and AIDS is no exception. The National Advisory Committee on AIDS, the new Expert Advisory Committee, the Canadian AIDS Society, and the Medical Research Council – not to mention the B.C. Civil Liberties Association – all have helpful advice for the Health Protection Branch in Canada, and the United States is certainly not behind us when it comes to forming such official and unofficial groups of pleaders. When they aren't managing the meddling of these groups, regulatory officials must deal with the omnipresent guest at any political feast – the political party in power. I mention this group because it is possible to forget that The Government (which can, as a matter of definition, have no other interest than the public interest) has an alter ego, and its alter ego has an agenda which is as distinctively private as those of the rest of the players confronting the regulatory authorities. There are definite and substantial electoral issues bound up in the management of AIDS, and any arm of the state charged with the governance of this disease must confront the claims made upon it by the party in power.

If all of this makes the work of the regulatory authorities seem difficult, then I have succeeded in conveying something of the truth. The FDA and the HPB must try to govern a set of forces that could produce, in the absence of a determined effort to protect the public interest, an essentially anarchic public health situation. And they must attempt to perform this mission with resources which always seem to be a step behind the demands placed upon them.

This needs to be borne in mind when frustration leads to a search for villains. The clinical and research group tends to see the regulatory authorities as a "bunch of officious bureaucrats who are too far removed from the world to feel the life and death realities facing the people they push around." The drug companies tend to see them as a "bunch of incompetent bureaucrats who could never make it out here in the real world with us, and who act out against their realization of this by pushing us around." These reflections, which were offered to me in private, are mercifully absent from the public face presented by these groups to the regulators. There, at least, something of the governmental power vested in them is responded to by fearful silence on the part of the researchers (who don't want to get on the wrong side of officials who will be adjudicating their submissions of experimental protocols for future research, and hence hold enormous sway over opportunities for professional advancement) and by downright fawning on the part of the drug companies, who look to the regulatory authorities for the license to sell their product – which is, in effect, the green light to get on with the task of reaping the rewards of their developmental work.

But just as reflection on the extremely complex character of the North American therapeutic system and the attempts to steer it with a marketing authority ought to keep us from simple-minded blame of the officials, drug company executives, and researchers caught up in it, it should also make us even more sympathetic of the plight of the catastrophically ill. In a system which is driven, at its core, by the lure of financial profit, and which is surrounded by a virtual galaxy of players – all of whom are trying to tilt the playing board in their direction (for the highest as well as the more ordinary of motives) – those who are simply trying to save their lives might be forgiven if they are in less than total awe of the rules of the game.

The rules need to be changed, and it is clear that the special challenge posed by AIDS is already moving the system in the direction of reform. However, sensible and lasting reform is going to demand more than the application of effective political pressure; it calls for the formulation of principles which can be institutionalized. The concept of catastrophic rights is meant to contribute to this task, and in the next section we shall explore some applications of the theory.

VIII.
Scenarios

THE PURPOSE of this section is to explore the practical significance of catastrophic rights in the context of some ideal scenarios. The scenarios approach has been chosen in order to avoid the need to make possibly contentious claims about real institutions, real drugs, and real people, while also giving concrete shape to the circumstances in which catastrophic rights ought to be recognized ... or denied.

First scenario:
promising
news from
the U.S.

IN READING the latest number of the *Journal of the National Cancer Institute* (one of the very many medical journals studied on a regular basis by AIDS people), Kevin discovers an article on a promising new therapy for an AIDS-related condition from which he suffers. The drug has not yet been approved for marketing in the U.S., and the application by the researchers and the sponsoring pharmaceutical company for exemption from the ordinary rigours of the pivotal clinical trials (through some program such as the Investigational New Drug category of the U.S. Food and Drug Administration which permits the clinical use of some drugs which show definite preliminary promise in the trial stage) has been denied. The point of the article read by Kevin is to provide information about the very promising indications that are emerging from the clinical trials, and to vent a portion of the frustration felt by the drug company and its investigators. Such controversy is a fairly regular feature of professional journals, and has come to be a more than ordinarily common feature of the discussion of new therapies for catastrophic illnesses.

Kevin's outlook is grim, and there are no established therapies available which offer any reasonable promise of either effective management or cure. He wants to try the new drug. He shows the article to his doctor and discusses the merits of trying such an unproven treatment. They decide that Kevin doesn't have a lot to lose from such a venture, since his present daunting prospect is for real discomfort and indignity as he inevitably moves towards death in the next year.

The physician telephones the sponsoring drug company in the U.S. and asks if they would be willing to make a supply of the drug available to her for use by her patient in Canada. They say they would. Would they require payment for the treatment? No, they would not. They do ask the physician to promise to keep very complete records of the administration of the treatment and its results, and to communicate the records to them. She agrees. The physician then telephones the Health Protection Branch in order to secure clearance from them to import and use the drug under the provisions of the Emergency Treatment sections of the Canadian Food and Drug Act.

As discussed earlier, the Emergency Treatment Provisions were not enacted with such a use in mind. Their function was originally conceived of in terms of the occasional need for drugs that are "orphaned" by the fact that the diseases for which they are indicated are too rare in Canada to justify the expense of seeking and gaining ordinary approval. But a legal loophole is a legal loophole, and all of the concerned parties in the access issue – including the HPB – have turned to the special provisions in search of a workable accomodation.

Should the HPB permit Kevin's physician to import and

administer the experimental drug? And more specifically, should Kevin's claim for a catastrophic right to try the drug play any part in the deliberations of the Branch in connection with this request?

I view this case as one that presents a model of the basic circumstances in which catastrophic rights make a distinctive claim which should be honoured. Kevin should not be prevented, by any agency of government, from obtaining and using an experimental drug under the circumstances of the scenario. The case would be otherwise if he were *not* catastrophically ill, but he is, and this fact should make a decisive difference.

There are several arguments against this conclusion which deserve consideration:

1. What about the responsibility of the HPB to safeguard the consumer interests of Canadians with respect to the safety and effectiveness of drugs? Shouldn't the Branch use its regulatory authority to protect Kevin from the possibly horrendous toxicity of a drug that has not yet satisfied internationally recognized standards of clinical testing?

As I argued earlier, in the section "Catastrophic Rights," the ordinary paternalism of the HPB must be modified in the face of a resolve to exercise a catastrophic right. I agree with all of those who stress the ability of toxicity to reveal itself late rather than early, and am mindful of the terrible force of "too late" where the use of powerful drugs is concerned. All things being equal, a conservative regulation of drugs is the appropriate governmental response to this painful fact of pharmaceutical life. But when, as PWAs so pointedly put it, the side-effect of their catastrophic illness is death, nothing is equal anymore. The treatment of terrible illness can medically and personally justify the acceptance of terrible risks. Chemotherapy, radiotherapy, and surgery all pose significant risks to health – and at least some of the damage they can cause is permanent and irreversible. Yet these negative effects may well be tolerable when balanced against a settled catastrophic prognosis. An unqualified goal of eliminating risk from therapy, no matter what the desperate patient may want, can be seen to be a misguided paternalism, given the accepted practice of using highly toxic therapies in those treatment environments which demand attention to the *ratio* of benefit to risk. The real question then is: where should we locate the authority to make the final judgment concerning risk/benefit in a catastrophic situation? The fundamental point of the doctrine of catastrophic rights is that, at least so far as paternalistic considerations go, such authority properly devolves upon the patient, in consultation with his physician ally.

2. *But what about the individual physician who retorts that all of the talk about risk-benefit ratios is very fine, except that what is strikingly at issue in the case of unapproved drugs is the absence of any scientifically established basis upon which to calculate these ratios? In such cases, the physician is not in a position to scientifically weigh the relative risks and benefits, and hence may reasonably judge that she hasn't satisfied the usual professional standards of care in avoiding causing harm to patients.*

This is a serious objection, and deserves a serious response from advocates of catastrophic rights. To begin with, let me state clearly that such a physician has a perfect right, as a medical professional, to refuse to provide treatment that she believes is more likely to harm than heal her patient. Nobody should suppose that a catastrophic right is a right to demand performance against professional conscience ... any more than one should suppose that the establishment of a right to abortion is a right to demand the cooperation of a medical professional against her conscience. However, just as a clinic might decide that it didn't want to hire an obstetrician who refused to do abortions, modern research hospitals may not wish to employ investigators who are inflexibly opposed to the recognition of catastrophic rights.

But the heart of the matter rests with the question of whether or not the recognition of catastrophic rights amounts to an abdication of the professional obligation to strive to avoid harm to one's patients. My view of this is that the professional responsibility to avoid harm must be assessed within a broad conception of the patient's welfare. For instance, and just to make the principle clear with a limiting case, few of us would accept, as a categorical limitation governing the provision of medical care, the rule that a physician cannot be involved in active euthanasia. Given a range of procedural protections, which I need not detail here, most of us would regard a physician as professionally correct in acceding to the clear request of her terminal patient for help in ending his life with dignity. The causing of death is ordinarily thought of as a very great – if not the greatest – harm that can be done to a human being, but in the case of euthanasia, we recognize that the refusal of a physician to take into consideration the deliberate and clearly stated desire of her patient is to refuse to accept, as a highly relevant factor in determining the patient's welfare, the patient's own personal assessment of how he wishes to spend his life. The patient may not want to continue to accept life on the terms that it is offered, and judge that now – as opposed to later – is the right time to quit.

The general point I want to make is that the deliberate therapeutic choices of patients are a highly relevant consideration when determining what is in their welfare. Human beings have bodies ... but to insist that persons are *only* flesh and blood would make even their clear refusal of treatment an irrelevant consideration, and, as we have discussed earlier, such a mistake could involve us not simply in a miscalculation of professional ethics, but in a criminal assault.

So when we consider the ethical concerns of medical professionals in connection with their cooperation in the provision of catastrophic therapies, our attention should centre on the intentionality of the patient's therapeutic choice. Is the patient reasonably well-informed? Does he understand the full range of possible consequences of the choice of an inadequately tested therapy? Has he been given a clear, complete, and objective account of his prognosis – with all of its uncertain positive as well as negative possibilities? If these matters have been professionally attended to, and the patient clearly and unequivocally elects to try a catastrophic therapy, he is giving a very clear indication of how he chooses to spend his life. To thwart him may, possibly, buy him extra time ... but, by definition, it is most improbable that it can save him from his catastrophic prognosis. The refusal to recognize such a patient's catastrophic right to try an untested therapy is based upon a narrow, and hence incorrect, assessment of the patient's welfare.

The answer to physicians' concerns about harming catastrophic patients must depend, in large part, upon what we think patients are. Advocates of catastrophic rights insist upon the humanity of patients as a highly relevant consideration in determining what constitutes harming or helping them. Human beings may be fairly said to create, with their choices, much of what is significant about their lives – just as a painter creates her work of art out of her brushstrokes. To thwart a catastrophic patient's deliberate intention to try an untested therapy visits a certain and considerable harm upon him which may not be overbalanced by whatever purely physical advantage he may realize as a result of doctor knowing best. Doctor may know best about bodies – but her professional obligation does not, interestingly, commit her to the care of mere bodies. It commits her to the care of persons.

This does *not* mean that a physician is always wrong to refuse to participate in the administration of a catastrophic treatment. A treating physician is the professional ally of her patient, not his creature. My point is, rather, that in weighing her professional judgment, a treating physician should properly give careful consideration to the informed, deliberate, and clearly stated therapeutic choices of her patient. These choices should be attended to not as something extrinsic to the professional medical task, but rather as an intrinsic element of any adequate assessment of the patient's welfare.

It is here that the distinction between the non-catastrophic versus catastrophic situation comes into sharp focus, for if Kevin's illness were migraine rather than AIDS, I would remain convinced of the merits of the case made out earlier for the social control of therapy. Kevin's catastrophic situation undercuts the general case for medical paternalism, because established medicine is simply without the means to guarantee that if it thwarts Kevin's therapeutic wishes, its doing so will result in "his own good." A catastrophic illness has a leveling influence on the relative claims to therapeutic competence of the physician and patient, and this justifies Kevin's claim to a greater measure of self-determination in his treatment.

3. What about quack, for-profit therapies, and the clinics which spring up to dispense them? When we consider the historical precedents for ripping-off the desperately ill, the principled position outlined above is surely a recipe for the introduction of additional miseries.

There is merit to this objection. But it is for this reason that Kevin's physician has been provided with an active role in this scenario – that is, a role that goes beyond the consultative one envisioned for her in the circumstance in which Kevin is self-acquiring and self-administering a novel therapy himself (as, for instance, in the use of mega-dosages of an over-the-counter medication untested for use on AIDS or its related conditions). In the scenario under consideration, it is Kevin's physician who is applying for the release of the drug, and the request is one which must pass the test of her professional judgment. Since that judgment is, as is the judgment of all physicians practicing in Canada, subject to review and censure by the various associations of medical professionals – which have charters from our government for this purpose – we have a measure of protection from quackery built into our scenario.

Some may argue that providing this veto to the physician is too paternalistic, and too disrespectful of the autonomy of the catastrophically ill. On the other hand, others may argue that Colleges of Physicians and Surgeons have proven themselves to be very ineffectual in policing their own ranks, and that if catastrophic rights are recognized, unscrupulous "AIDS Doctors" will quickly establish themselves as top money-earners in those provinces which have weak professional associations. I take both contentions seriously; indeed, it is the plausibility of both of them which has convinced me that the middle course of providing a veto to the attending physician is the best course to follow. Then, if the professional Colleges don't do their job, we should address that as a problem. And if physicians are insensitive to the therapeutic choices of their patients as an element of their patients' welfare, we should address that as a problem as well. But neither of these possibilities should be taken as sufficient reason for denying catastrophic rights.

4. What about the responsibility of the HPB to protect the health of all Canadians by preserving an orderly system of experimental trials in which the safety and effectiveness of therapies can be definitely determined? How are we ever going to manage the illness Kevin suffers from if we permit the emergence of a form of therapeutic anarchy?

The answer to this is rooted in the bald fact that most trials of most therapies don't occur in Canada, but in the largest potential markets for them, in such countries as the U.S. In the case at hand, the pivotal clinical trials of what the FDA terms Stage Three are already in process, and the sponsoring company has no intention of initiating a duplicate set of such expensive trials in Canada. They will simply apply for marketing privileges from the HPB when the American work is completed, offering the records of the trials which satisfied the FDA in support of their application. Thus, in this instance – as in many related ones in the real world – the responsibility of the HPB to protect the Canadian ability to advance medical knowledge by protecting the ability to do genuinely scientific research is, as a practical consideration, quite beside the facts of pharmaceutical life.

5. Or is it? Shouldn't we anticipate, if such relief from the regulations became a general practice, that catastrophically ill patients would flock to Canada in order to enjoy the exercise of catastrophic rights? And wouldn't they simply represent an additional burden on our already straining health care system?

I would respond to these questions with one of my own: would it be appropriate for us to withhold a right from Canadians, that we believed was legitimate for them to claim, on the grounds that if we honoured the right Canada would be a more attractive country? This would be an obnoxious argument if offered in connection with established rights such as the right to due process of law; why should we accept it in the case of *any* right? A variant of this "medical refugee" argument would be that honouring catastrophic rights in cases such as Kevin's might actually destroy an important element of the circumstances that make the scenario sympathetic to catastrophic claims in the first place. That is, wouldn't it be likely that subjects in American trials would move to Canada in order to escape the possibility of being an element of the control arm in the American study? And if they did move in numbers significant enough to damage the ability of American researchers to determine the safety and effectiveness of new drugs, wouldn't this undercut our previous argument about the relaxed obligation of the HPB to protect our ability to do genuinely scientific research?

There are essentially two responses to be made to this possible threat. First, it is very difficult to assess the likelihood of such an exodus of the catastrophically ill under the conditions of the scenario. My personal belief is that it would be limited to a marginal phenomenon, and hence wrong to allow it to drive policy formation. Secondly, if I was proven wrong, and an influx of the catastrophically ill threatened to overwhelm the Canadian healthcare system, I would be among the first to urge that it was time to think again. The central idea behind my formulation of catastrophic rights is to give them that measure of force that is consistent with the protection of the vital public health interests of Canadians. As with other rights, catastrophic rights are not absolute. The emergence of conditions that would make their recognition tantamount to seriously harming our ability to continue to protect the health of Canadians would define their reasonable limit.

However, we shouldn't neglect the possibility that at least some catastrophically ill patients enter into strictly controlled trials with a genuine willingness to be one of the control group – if that is the luck of the draw. We shouldn't prejudge the question of whether the commitment of genuinely uncoerced subjects would disappear if there were a chance of successfully claiming a catastrophic right to the drug under trial. We will return to this very important consideration in the next scenario.

*Second scenario:
promising
news from
home*

KEVIN has weathered several bouts of AIDS-related illness. He learns from other PWAs that the City Hospital is running an experimental trial of a new therapy for the respiratory illness that has been most damaging to him. He wants to try the drug, but isn't willing to join a trial where he will have only a 50 percent chance of getting the new drug instead of the standard therapy which has failed him. Kevin isn't confident that he can survive his next bout of illness, and believes that it makes more sense for him to risk the possibility that the drug doesn't work, or even the possibility that it hastens his death. He makes out his case to his doctor, who cautiously agrees with the logic of Kevin's contention that there must be *some* reason to attach promise or hope to the treatment, else why would the hospital be experimenting with it?

Kevin's doctor telephones the multinational pharmaceutical company which is sponsoring the trial of the new drug. The company is willing to provide a supply of the drug for free if Kevin's doctor will maintain careful records of the administration of the treatment, along with Kevin's response to it, and communicate those records to the company at regular intervals. The drug company makes this offer on condition that Kevin's physician is able to obtain the HPB's approval of the arrangement. The company naturally does not want to do anything that would disturb the Branch's approval of the experimental trial that is in process, since the satisfaction of the regulatory requirements is an essential step in the procedure that could result in the all-important approval to market the drug. Thus, Kevin and his physician face an "it's all right with us if it's all right with them" situation. Kevin's doctor applies to the Branch for the necessary permission to try the drug.

I would contend that the HPB should recognize Kevin's catastrophic right to try the new drug. However, and at the same time, the Branch has a continuing obligation to strive to protect the health of Canadians by preserving our ability to determine the safety and effectiveness of therapies – including therapies for the treatment of catastrophic illnesses. The question then is: should Kevin's catastrophic right trump the public interests sought by the HPB in the scenario under consideration? In answering this question I will refer back to my statement of the principle which I offered earlier as governing the scope of catastrophic rights: that is, they ought to be as broad as possible to reflect the respect of Canadians for personal self-determination in that which affects us most personally and intimately, and as narrow as is necessary to leave materially undisturbed the vital public interests served by the social control of therapies.

How can such conflicts be resolved? Our long experience with the logic of rights claims provides us with at least a good beginning in answering this question. Democratic governments are familiar with individual rights claims, and have evolved a fairly robust system for dealing with them. The main point to be grasped is that an individual's expression of a right has a presumptive claim to recognition in the absence of any countervailing case against it being made out by government. In default of its making out a good case for some superseding obligation – such as the responsibility to attend to a vital public interest – government has an obligation to recognize the claim of an individual right as dominating ordinary legal or policy considerations.

Thus, in considering whether or not Kevin's catastrophic right has a trumping force in the scenario under consideration, we should not proceed as if an obligation to make out his case rests in the first instance with Kevin, but rather as if government has an obligation to make out its case for depriving him of it. This may seem like a mere subtlety, and, given the opportunity to canvass the full range of argument available in such a conflict, it cannot be supposed to make an enormous difference to the ultimate outcome of adjudication. It does, however, ensure that the appropriate deliberations actually take place, and that the arguments get a public hearing that is subject to some form of appellate review. In the final analysis, the routine provision of such a process, undertaken against the background of the presumptive force of individual rights, is one of the most important moral achievements of the democracies.

Putting the onus on the government does not mean that the government is without a case (or cases) to make. In the scenario before us, the first response of the Health Protection Branch would certainly be to refer us yet again to its general and overarching obligation to protect the vital health interests of all Canadians. We need scientifically reliable information about new drugs if we are to discharge our obligation to the generations of ill persons we know must follow the particular patients confronting us at any given moment. A sound public health program must be wide-ranging, with the farthest-seeing conception of Canadian health interests at its centre.

Kevin appreciates the force of this argument, but he has a vexingly sophisticated command of the literature in the experimental drug field, and documents the existence of no less than five formal trials of his chosen drug that are in progress in the United States. These formal trials, the experimental protocols of which have been approved by the FDA, are designed to provide scientifically reliable indications of safety and effectiveness. But are *six* scientifically rigorous trials of a single promising drug for a catastrophic illness necessary? One might quickly respond that when such significant health issues are at stake, the more science the better. All things being equal, this is certainly so. But Kevin's claim of a catastrophic right changes all of that.

If the HPB is to justify depriving Kevin of his right, they must make out a case that such a step is necessary in order to preserve our ability to scientifically ascertain the safety and effectiveness of an investigational drug. This refers to the general argument that if they can't protect our ability to do science, they cannot discharge their obligation to protect the vital health interests of Canadians. The experimental trials of the new drug at Kevin's hospital may perhaps be fairly said to *contribute* to medical knowledge. They may not, however, be accurately said to be *necessary* to determine whether or not the drug is safe and effective. That question is going to be answered, one way or the other, by the American trials. The government's case for overriding Kevin's catastrophic right to the drug must be said to rest on the importance of the Canadian contribution that is being made by the trial at City Hospital – and it is an inadequate case.

The case is inadequate because it is contending not with an individual interest, but with a catastrophic right. A vital public interest makes a compelling case against an opposing individual right, but it denies the individual right only if the vital component of the public interest cannot be protected by less drastic means. As I pointed out in the section on "Science and Rights," a democratic government has an obligation to try to get around the denial of the individual rights of its citizens, and if it can't be avoided, to cut into them as little as possible. As little as possible means just up to that point necessitated by the obligation to provide for a vital public purpose. There is, therefore, an element of proportionality in the overriding force of a vital public interest *vis à vis* a contending individual right. It is not enough for the Canadian trials of the new drug to produce medically significant scientific progress. They must be an indispensable element of the scientific effort to determine efficacy and safety if they are to legitimately override Kevin's catastrophic right to try the drug. I hasten to emphasize that none of this amounts to a denial of the right of Canadian researchers to conduct scientific trials of the new drug. That is never at issue – unless, of course, one assumes that the coercion of human subjects is a necessary condition of the conduct of all scientific trials. What *is* at issue here is the practical significance of Kevin's claim of a catastrophic right in the specific circumstances of the scenario.

But what of the obvious response that modern science works systemically, and depends upon the aggregation of many individual investigational efforts in order to work its syncretic magic? No single trial is usually an absolutely necessary element of scientific work, which is more and more commonly transnational. But if catastrophic rights are successfully urged against each of the trials in isolation, without consideration for the way in which they fit together to form a larger whole, the system will break down, and the vital public health interests connected with its success will go unprovided for.

I agree with the description of the systemic character of modern research. I even agree, in principle, with the objection to a process by which catastrophic rights might damage our ability to make medical progress by gobbling up our scientific capabilities one bite at a time. What this general response to the proportionality argument misses, however, is that national borders still form significant seams in the transnational fabric of experimental trials. They do so because the provision and protection of individual rights is a political commitment of a sovereign nation – that is, a promise made by a human community with the means to keep it.

It is well to remember that the protection of civil rights is not something that is done "against" the power of the state. In the final analysis, individual rights can only thrive in a human community that has the political will to use its corporate power to provide for and maintain them. They don't fool around a lot with talk about the rights of PWAs in Russia or China. One of the virtues of conceiving of the drug access issue in terms of rights, is that it makes it possible to harness some of the existing moral resources of our system of government. Seeing this issue as just another instance of "getting government off the backs of the people" is, in my view, to see it in hopelessly narrow terms. Only a democratic state is likely to care for, and have the means to provide for, the rights of catastrophically ill people. The task isn't to get governments out of the picture, but to put them into the right part of the picture.

In this case, the Canadian government is responsible for both the protection of Canadian interests, and the rights of Canadian citizens. If the sacrifice of Kevin's catastrophic right can be avoided without significant damage to medical science in Canada, then the Canadian government has an obligation to give precedence to his claim.

My analysis of this scenario is unlikely to be welcome to some of the Canadian researchers who want to professionally engage the challenge of AIDS in a cooperative effort with their American colleagues. All things being equal, their keenness to contribute is admirable and deserves nothing but encouragement and support. My present point, however, is that the introduction of a catastrophic right means that things are no longer at all equal, and the individual right of the patient takes precedence over the professional welfare of the researchers.

In this connection I stress that I am *not* accusing either Canadian researchers, or the HPB, of insensitivity to the plight of catastrophic patients. Canada has a large population of PWAs, and professionals at all levels of our therapeutic system quite appropriately desire to be nationally active in combatting a disease which has no respect for international borders. What I am claiming, however, is that in a case in which a drug is already the subject of a full range of scientific trials in another country, the government of Canada is not justified in denying the catastrophic rights of Canadians who wish to try it. I emphasize that this claim does not ignore the fact of the transnational character of the AIDS virus; indeed, it underscores the irrelevance of considerations such as national pride in dealing with as serious a threat as AIDS, and as important a matter as individual patients' rights.

In connection with the issue of national pride, it might be argued against my position that it could well have the effect of relegating Canada to the status of a research backwater in the fight against catastrophic illnesses. If Kevin's catastrophic right is honoured, why wouldn't all those who entered the City Hospital trial in the hope that they might be one of the recipients of the active agent, rather than a member of the control, simply claim a similar right and wreck the experiment? We will return later to a careful consideration of this supposition about the behaviour of research subjects, but let me simply allow it as a fact for the purposes of the present scenario. What then? I would respond that, if anything, an acceptance of my analysis of this scenario (including the threat of defecting research subjects) should spur Canadian researchers and regulators to aspire to a more innovative role than simple replication of a coercive system of experimentation. The fact that we are without a national car is not seen as a serious threat to our identity as a distinct and sovereign country, and if necessary, we should be willing to sacrifice a measure of nationalist pride in our research program rather than the civil rights of catastrophic patients.

One final point is raised by Kevin in justifying his claim to a catastrophic right, and it is a point that directs our attention to one of the junctures of politics and science in the trial of experimental drugs. At the present time, virtually all subjects for the trial of experimental drugs are recruited with the understanding that two most significant considerations shape their situation and choice:

1. The only way to get the experimental drug is to join its trial as a subject.

2. About half the subjects joining the trial will get not the experimental drug, but a control drug – either the established therapy or a placebo, depending on the experiment.

This makes agreement to the second consideration follow naturally upon agreement to the first. One of the most important rationales for this system of recruitment has been the importance of maintaining subject discipline. How do you persuade catastrophically ill human beings to become guinea pigs in a blinded experiment in which they stand only a 50 percent chance of getting the treatment they want? *One* – and I stress that it is but one – way of accomplishing this is to restrict the availability of the new drug to the experimental setting. Then, the desperation of patients can be transformed into an important element of their willingness to comply with the trial conditions. They are made a deal they can't refuse. The justification of this coercive system, its apologists contend, rests with the needs of medical science. Unless those needs are met, the ability of the medical establishment to provide the treatments we depend upon will be compromised.

Because the justification of this coercive (or imperfectly voluntary, or – as one investigator straight-facedly put it to me – "opportunistic in the service of a higher good") recruitment of experimental subjects rests upon an empirical claim – the claim that coercion represents the only way of ensuring the subject discipline required of genuinely scientific experimentation – it also suggests the possibility of confirmation or disconfirmation of that claim. What if it isn't true? And what if its being true or false depends upon the political and moral commitment of persons rather than simply some natural feature of the world? That is: what if there were catastrophic patients willing to enter experimental trials even though their right to the experimental drug didn't depend upon their becoming experimental subjects? And what if there were sufficient numbers of such patients to make at least some controlled experimentation of catastrophic treatments possible, while preserving completely voluntary conditions of participation and exclusion?

Empirical questions can only be answered by testing the world, and the answer to the empirical question posed by Kevin is of tremendous importance. The provision of justice, as against the inflicting of injustice, depends upon our getting an answer to it. In such a circumstance, even a minimal recognition of catastrophic rights requires that we discontinue the routine use of coercive recruitment strategies until we know that they are really necessary. If it is true that genuinely voluntary trials can be successful, then we shall have provided for the exercise of an important right at absolutely no cost to our ability to do science. Indeed, we may discover that the creation of an *esprit* that more closely links the research community with its subjects, will benefit at least some studies that depend heavily upon subject discipline. And if our best efforts sometimes fail to turn up the needed subjects, then we may, with somewhat better conscience, revert to some version of the devil we know.

Third scenario:
the limits of
catastrophic
rights

KEVIN is invited by his doctor to participate in the trial of an experimental drug at City Hospital. The drug has been developed by a small Canadian pharmaceutical company, and has shown no sign of toxicity and very promising anti-viral indications in its trials in animals. Of course, only carefully designed trials of the drug can possibly settle the issue of its safety and effectiveness in humans, so a small group of twenty patients (small enough so as to minimize the number of persons potentially harmed by the experiment, but large enough to provide real information) is being formed to take the drug through the next appropriate step. The HPB has approved the experimental protocol, and the drug company is sponsoring (i.e. paying for) the trials. The drug is unavailable anywhere else in the world; indeed, it is so novel that it only exists in sufficient quantities to run the City Hospital experiment that Kevin has been invited to join.

Kevin is desperately ill, and his doctor has suggested to him that he is unlikely to live for more than six months. He wants to be certain that he isn't getting a placebo (or the established therapy which has already failed to help him) rather than the trial drug, and claims a catastrophic right to use the drug outside the projected trial. Kevin recognizes that the likelihood that this last hope will work out is very, very slight. But he isn't making an argument that is grounded in the likelihood of this particular experimental drug being successful; he is making an argument that rests upon his enhanced claim to therapeutic autonomy. Kevin's doctor is sufficiently sympathetic to this argument to telephone the drug company and request a supply of the drug.

The company refuses, pointing out that the drug is extremely expensive to produce, and that the decision to seek cheaper means of making it will wait upon the results of the City Hospital trial. If the drug shows real promise, the development of more efficient means of manufacturing it will be energetically explored; otherwise, the company will cut its losses and look at the possibility of sponsoring other drugs in other trials. In the meantime, however, they cannot honour Kevin's claim to a catastrophic right, and they add the opinion that even if they could (i.e. if there was a surplus of the drug over what was needed for the trial), they don't believe that they are under any obligation to threaten the existence of their trial (evoking again the threat of

defecting experimental subjects) by supplying the drug to someone who has not accepted the conditions of the experimental
situation in which they are willing to provide it.

First of all, what about the company's claim that since they
don't have any surplus drug, they can't provide any for Kevin?
They could possibly reduce the number of persons in the experimental trial by one, and thus recover enough drug to supply
compassionate treatment for Kevin. My view is that Kevin's
right to have a chance to obtain the drug doesn't outweigh the
rights of those who have agreed to enter the trial. What is more, I
find it hard to believe that the consequences of Kevin's getting
the drug under this scenario would fall narrowly on him. The
drug is scarce, and the trial is already at the small end of the
useful limit. Excluding one "active" subject from the trial would
damage its ability to provide a clear indication of the safety and
effectiveness of the experimental drug. Besides, even if only a
few subjects defect so as to be certain of obtaining the drug as
Kevin had, the trial would be doomed, and the possibility of
advancing the search for AIDS treatments would be to that extent
diminished.

But what of the drug company's opinion that they would not
rest under any obligation to provide the drug, even if there were a
surplus of it? My view of this is that they might be morally obligated if recognizing catastrophic rights in such circumstances
didn't interfere with the successful mounting and completion of
the trial. Even if this were so, however, I wouldn't think them
under any legal obligation to be responsive. Legality becomes an
issue only when we turn to the role of the HPB, because the
Branch is an agent of the government administering Canadian
statute law and regulations. All such law rests under the superior
authority of the Charter of Rights and Freedoms, and can
possibly be reviewed by a Canadian court and found to be
unconstitutional.

Let us imagine that, in the scenario we are considering, the
pharmaceutical company was willing to provide Kevin with the
trial drug – either because they had a slight surplus, or because
they believed that his claim took precedence over the importance

of the trial. Responsibility would then devolve squarely upon the HPB. My view of the case would be that the same considerations that ought to persuade the company to refuse Kevin should operate at the governmental level of the Branch. The HPB would be able to make a case for an overriding vital public health interest in maintaining the conditions that make the trial possible. We would be at the limit of catastrophic rights.

Fourth scenario: who pays?

KEVIN'S buying club learns that there have been remarkably promising Phase III results (efficacy trials) of a new anti-retroviral drug in the United States. There are no parallel trials of the drug underway or proposed in Canada, and there is no question that the investigation in the United States could succeed or fail because of anything done or left undone here. Kevin's club approaches the American drug company through some of the physicians that have undertaken to advise them, and learns that the company is willing to make any amount of the drug available to patients here – just as long as they are willing to pay for it. The drug will cost about $1000 per month per patient, and many of the members of Kevin's club cannot afford it. Needless to say, many of them have been unable to work since the onset of their symptoms. However, a very large proportion of those who can no longer work have also been able to maintain a measure of financial independence by resorting to their savings, by drastically reducing their standard of living, and by liquidating some of their assets; that is, they have not resorted to the public purse in the form of welfare payments.

This last consideration is important, because the provincial government pays for the pharmaceutical expenses of patients who are the clients of its welfare system. Thus, many of the members of Kevin's buying club are in his position: they have been able – through their own efforts and those of their friends – to forestall the indignity of "going on welfare," but they must now give up this important foundation of their self-esteem if they are to be able to try the very promising drug which might save or prolong their lives. What is worse, they understand that in the face of a systemically debilitating disease such as AIDS, the ability to maintain a measure of independence and self-respect may be one of the most important elements of a patient's ability to muster the spirit to survive. (In so describing Kevin's predicament, I don't want to be interpreted as criticizing those members of the community who have been forced to apply for welfare. Rather, I want to concentrate on the very real interest of Kevin and others to stave off this eventuality.)

As in so many other like instances, the government's regulations permit a fairly broad range of discretionary latitude in paying for drug expenses. Although the general form of the scheme is one in which a distinction is drawn between those drugs which are an integral part of a medical procedure (i.e. roughly all of the drugs taken while hospitalized), and those which are not (i.e. roughly all of the drugs you take once you go home), in practice the government has shown understanding of the special circumstances of catastrophic patients. Organ transplant recipients require a very expensive immunosuppressant called cyclosporin, and the government pays for it. If they did not, some individuals and families might be forced into bankruptcy in order to purchase the drug for even a fraction of the time period during which it is needed.

The situation is further complicated by the long-standing policy of the government not to pay for treatment with experimental drugs. Indeed, it is unlawful to offer such experimental drugs for sale in Canada. In this connection, it is important to remember that the method used by the HPB to control prescription drugs is to control the market for them. In circumstances such as the one under consideration in this scenario, the established practice has been to require the drug company to supply the drug on a compassionate basis (if the HPB agrees), pending the marketing approval of the drug. The drug company must wait for the drug to be licensed for sale before it can begin to make money from it.

But what if, as is the case in this scenario, the experimental drug becomes the international standard of care before the completion of any of the usual trials? What if the very catastrophic nature of the illness for which the drug is to be used is such that virtually everyone involved recognizes that to forestall general use of it in the face of early, yet compelling, evidence of its safety and efficacy would be immoral? How will the drug company satisfy the regulatory preconditions of sale and profit? And what is the proper response of government to the claim of a catastrophic right to receive the drug?

There are really two questions here, and it is important to distinguish them. Firstly, there is the matter of whether or not Kevin has a catastrophic right to the experimental drug *with respect to the question of whether or not the Health Protection Branch should permit its importation and use.* Our answer to that question, as per our discussion of a relevantly similar case in Scenario Two, is an unequivocal "Yes." But secondly, there is the pressingly (depressingly?) practical matter of payment. If the HPB will not permit the experimental drug to be sold in Canada, catastrophic patients will be denied its legal use. And if the HPB permits its sale – under some extraordinary provision, but the provincial governments do not undertake to pay for its use, then many patients will face an impossible practical obstacle to their use of the treatment.

There are terrible difficulties here. I would argue, in connection with the question of payment for the use of experimental drugs, the importance of distinguishing between legal and moral rights . . . and legal and moral duties. Although I find the question of the legal duty of government to pay for experimental therapies to be problematical, I am much less diffident about the moral rights of catastrophic patients in this connection, and the correlative moral duties of government when confronted by them.

Stepping out of the fictitious setting of the scenario, at the time of writing we face a situation in British Columbia in which the provincial government has refused to pay for the use of AZT by AIDS patients. The government has made much of the fact that its legal advisers have assured it that it rests under no *legal* obligation to pay for the use of this drug, the regulatory status of which is still unclear. The B.C. Civil Liberties Association and the Provincial Ombudsman both urged the government to relent, pointing out that there were no relevant moral or administrative distinction to be drawn between the chemotherapies used by our Cancer Control Agency and cyclosporin as used by transplant recipients – all paid for by our medical plan. Why risk even the appearance of discrimination against AIDS patients, when it is so easy to understand that precisely the same issues of individual ability to pay, conjoined with catastrophic consequences, were present in the case of AZT as were in the cases of cyclosporin or the chemotherapies? In an unprecedented move, even the Minister of Health's own Expert Advisory Committee on AIDS unanimously echoed – in a confidential document which was duly leaked – the civil libertarians' arguments, and recommended immediate funding of AZT treatments.

No clear response to the case for funding was ever offered publicly, other than the rather smug insistence that there was no *legal* obligation to pay – a contention presently being tested in the courts by the Vancouver Persons With Aids Society. (There was a foolish attempt to suggest that the government did not want B.C. to turn into a "mecca for AIDS sufferers." This is a rather silly red herring, given that every other province in Canada already pays for the use of AZT by AIDS people, and given that B.C. is the most seriously affected province in terms of known levels of seroprevalence.)

The AZT situation in B.C. is especially significant. It represents a limiting case for those Canadians who believe that it doesn't make sense for governments to pay for the use of experimental drugs by the catastrophically ill. The general principle that has driven the Canadian health scheme for the last couple of generations is that the provision of health care ought to be removed far enough from the anarchic forces of the marketplace so that Canadians will not be deprived of essential medical services because of their inability to pay for them. The great idea was – and is – that whatever our general fondness for the bracing effects of the discipline of the market, we regarded the sickroom as an inappropriate and cruel arena for their operation. Payment for the ordinary range of pharmaceuticals by the user has been regarded as the sort of extra that didn't threaten the basic principle of our medical system. However, user-payment for very expensive drugs which are an integral part of a treatment regime for a life-threatening illness cannot be reconciled with those fundamental principles.

AZT was an experimental drug that became the international standard of care long before it satisfied the regulatory requirements of virtually any First World country. If advancements in the development of drugs proceed as quickly and as successfully as we must all hope that they shall, it is inevitable that other drugs will emerge whose safety and efficacy are clearly evident far in advance of their satisfaction of ordinary regulatory requirements. I believe that government has a moral duty to provide such drugs on a free basis to the catastrophically ill, and I also believe that to do so may very well hasten the process of discovering treatments for the most expensive of the diseases that confront our necessarily limited health-care resources.

I offer this more as a reflection than a confident prediction, but I don't think that it is an empty notion. One of the great obstacles to medical advancement in general, and in the case of certain catastrophic illnesses especially, is the money needed to properly mount very large clinical trials of experimental drugs. In the case of a disease such as AIDS, the damage done to the immune system, along with the concomitant damage to vital organs by opportunistic infections and tumours, underscores the importance of a multi-faceted approach to cure or even very effective palliation. As Jerome Groopman of Harvard has pointed out, AIDS "does not play by the conventional rules of drug development":

> If many vital systems are deteriorating concurrently, it is quite difficult to distinguish the metabolism of the drug and its toxic effects from the symptoms of the disease itself. Since many AIDS sufferers are also intravenous drug addicts, sorting out the damage done by the disease from the damage done by the illicit drugs is difficult at best. Nonetheless, we must respond to the real world of the disorder; the complexity of the disease should not bar the patient from access to potentially life-saving therapy.
>
> "Rx For The FDA," *The New Republic*, Feb. 13, 1989

The form of science done in the controlled experimental setting is one that strives to simplify the "question" asked of the
trial by careful limitation of the medical condition of the subjects
– the better to get a definitive answer. Such science is the foundation of the largest part of the success of medicine, but the
answers it gleans to its "simple" questions are going to stand
very much in need of confirmation in the rough and tumble of the
inextricably complicated clinical setting presented to us by typical AIDS patients. These considerations suggest that honouring
catastrophic rights at the regulative level (remembering, of
course, that such rights have limits – as discussed above), and
footing the bill for the provision of promising therapies to catastrophic patients *in the context of* well-funded and administered
clinical studies, could materially shorten the time needed to find
effective cures for ruinously expensive catastrophic illnesses
such as AIDS.

Fifth scenario:
who is
catastrophically
ill?

KEVIN has recently been informed by his physician that he
is HIV positive. It was nagging anxiety rather than illness that
led him to take the test, and now he knows the worst.

His worst, however, doesn't look so bad over at the Persons
With Aids Society – a group which he joined immediately upon
learning that he had seroconverted. Those members of the
Society who already have developed AIDS live in a state of
medical siege. They are truly embattled. Asymptomatic seropositives such as Kevin are the new recruits to the AIDS battle, and
they can look forward to as much as a decade – or even longer –
before they will be in the frontlines with their first opportunistic
illness. Indeed, the early 1990 statistics place the median period
of latency or incubation of HIV at about nine to ten years. Kevin
places the most likely date of his infection at two years ago, giv-

ing him a statistically supported hope of seven more years before he develops AIDS.

Kevin learns of an investigation of a new drug at City Hospital. It is an anti-viral which is going for the "brass ring" of HIV therapies – a knockout blow to the virus itself. If it works as its sponsors hope it will, those who use it will be literally cured. The drug represents one of the newest waves of AIDS research, which is the effort to destroy the virus before it has a chance to turn the immune system of a PWA into a virtual Humpty Dumpty. Those of us who have not entered that Other Kingdom of PWAs can conjure up only the faintest imaginative sense of what such a drug means to Kevin. It is a potential life-saver.

Kevin talks to his physician about the drug trial, and they apply to the investigators for a copy of the experimental protocol. Kevin fits all of the inclusion criteria, but is brought up short by the fact that the experimental design calls for half of the subjects to be randomized into a placebo-controlled arm. Kevin doesn't want half of whatever chance the drug promises; he wants all of whatever chance there is for him to be freed from the curse of living on borrowed time. He and his physician decide to demand that the investigators provide an open arm for the trial, so that the catastrophically ill can exercise their right to try the drug without taking the chance of being randomized into the control.

Here is the rub. From the point of view of the investigators, the new drug is a potential treatment only for those who are *not yet* catastrophically ill. They argue that it is precisely those features of Kevin's medical situation that fit him for the trial which exclude him from the category of the catastrophically ill.

The new drug holds out promise of being a lifesaver, but it is a life-saver that has been specifically designed to be worn by, and can almost certainly only possibly save, those who are not yet in the water. Kevin isn't sick yet, will probably not be ill for several more years, and may – for all we know for certain – never fall ill at all. He may die of some other cause before he ever develops AIDS (plenty can happen in five or more years), or he may simply be one of a vanishingly small and lucky number in

whom the disease is never activated. He may even be the benefi-
ciary of a medical break-through. Indeed, his life expectancy –
even without any effective treatment – is said by some epidemi-
ologists to be comparable to that of a middle-aged man who has
survived a first major heart attack.

The results of the animal trials and preliminary human trials
have provided strong medical indications that drug X would be
fatal to a person with AIDS. In this respect, it has one of the most
common features of powerful anti-virals: extreme toxicity. In
fact, the poisonous side-effects of the new drug are still only
partly understood or estimated, and it is simply not known
whether an asymptomatic seropositive can take enough of it for
long enough to knock out the immunodeficiency virus before the
side-effects kill him. Thus, it is a genuine toss-up whether
someone in Kevin's position should take it or leave it. Drug X is
a real "kill or cure" toss of the dice, and represents a terrible
gamble for someone who is not yet actually sick. The point of the
experimental trial of X is to find volunteers who will help medical researchers learn more about the drug while they let random
chance determine what no one can know beforehand . . . what's
the best bet for the subjects who fit the inclusion criteria, drug X
or nothing?

The investigators have several arguments in support of their
position.

1. If the concept of catastrophic illness is allowed to balloon to
the point that it includes asymptomatic seropositives, it has
parted company with our ordinary intuition of what constitutes a
catastrophe. All of us, for instance, are going to die from what
might be called the disease or condition of aging. This may well
be a tragedy, but it is not a catastrophe; that is, it is not an erup-
tion of some emergent and terrible threat into the normal course
of our lives. Insistence upon an expansive conception of catastrophic illness can only serve, by weakening the connection it
makes with our intuitions, to weaken the claim of a catastrophic
right to therapeutic self-determination – a right which is far from
well-established even in its most conservative form.

2. The ordinary and limited paternalism embodied in the regulation of drugs for non-catastrophic illnesses has a powerful

claim to our attention in this context. Asymptomatic seropositives may well stampede in the direction of a deadly drug-of-the-month which could kill all or most of those who take it. Unless we believe that medical science is not our best chance of finding an effective treatment for AIDS, we must recognize that the provision of catastrophic rights can never be expected to be a net medical benefit to those who claim and use them. The provision of such a right to those who are not yet facing proximate death may be seen to be, in this context, the irresponsible abdication of our power to protect public health.

3. An expansive definition of catastrophic illness runs into another moral and political roadblock. To the extent that we limit the ability of medical scientists to ask and answer important questions about experimental drugs in the context of carefully controlled trials, we place a significant obstacle in the way of those scientists' efforts to find safe and effective treatments. I have argued that a catastrophic right goes a long way toward overriding ordinary considerations of public interest and responsibility, but insisting on a tremendously expansive definition of catastrophic illness may lead us in the direction of giving far too little weight to the rights of (and our correlative obligations to) those generations of future patients whose welfare depends upon our doing our best to find treatments for their illnesses before they get them.

Kevin is not without a comeback to these arguments. To begin with, there is an important asymmetry between his statistical situation and the statistical situation of a recovered heart-attack victim. We may in good conscience say, to the heart attack victim, that he has a real chance of never dying from a heart attack. That is, he does not rest under a practically certain death sentence from cardiac failure. Maybe he'll die tomorrow (becoming a skewing influence on the statistics), but it may be just as likely that he will live out something like his normal lifespan before succumbing. We cannot honestly say anything like that to Kevin. It may take some indeterminate and even a considerable period of time, but it is a virtual certainty that he will have his life cut short by AIDS.

Besides, PWAs have recognized a certain artificiality in the division between the asymptomatic and the symptomatic among themselves. One does not, after all, have to have AIDS to be discriminated against as an AIDS person. One need only, as are all those infected with the disease – asymptomatic or not – be regarded as infectious with it. PWA Societies throughout North America have become convinced of the political and moral reasonableness of opening their membership to anyone who describes himself as HIV positive. Making common cause with everyone in the same boat with themselves has given their movement more members and proportionally more power, and it would be very awkward for them to permit the reintroduction of a distinction which they are reaping the success of having set aside. It would be uncomfortably like having first and second class PWAs: those with catastrophic rights, and those who continue to be denied them.

Many PWAs and their advocates fear that as more and more research centres on the asymptomatic seropositive, the therapeutic authorities will be willing to cut loose those who have developed AIDS. This will be done, it is argued, not so much out of respect for the catastrophic rights of those who are desperately ill, but in order to perfect and legitimize the maintenance of complete control over the asymptomatic seropositives – and hence over the serious scientific action. Given the record of the therapeutic authorities, and the historical record of the past decade, this can hardly be dismissed as baseless paranoia.

Still, my personal conviction is that the investigators have the stronger case. If there is to be content to the notion of a catastrophic illness – if it is to really mean *some*thing – then it cannot be or mean *every*thing. My suggestion is that it makes sense, in early 1990, to consider only those who have already developed an AIDS-related illness to be catastrophically ill, along with everyone in whom surrogate markers suggest the imminence of such opportunistic illness. Such a distinction does not throw the asymptomatic seropositives to the wolves. In fact, there is a good case to be made that granting catastrophic rights to those who are not facing a genuinely catastrophic situation exposes them to the possibility of becoming therapeutic "adventurers" before such a dangerous course makes sense. Besides, persons living with AIDS can be counted upon to bring all of their considerable medical and political expertise to a watching brief on experimentation that concerns their brothers and sisters among the asymptomatics. There are, we should not forget, many more patients' rights than the catastrophic variety, and all PWAs will continue to be energetic claimants of them. In fact, I think that it is now fair to say that relations between the therapeutic authorities and all human experimental subjects have been altered forever by the efforts of AIDS people. Viewed from such a perspective, this essay is not so much an attempt to make something happen as it is an effort to make sense of a vigorous process that is well begun.

IX.
Doing
the Right
Thing

NORTH AMERICAN therapeutic authorities have never been categorically opposed to the special release of unapproved drugs. But when they have permitted exceptions to their regulatory restrictions, they have understood the transaction in terms of *compassion*, rather than in terms of *rights*. The Investigational New Drug program in the U.S., and the Emergency Drug Release Program in Canada are, both in their self-descriptive literature and in the minds of those who administer them, programs for the release of drugs as a special form of kindness. This conceptual framework has been of central significance in the struggle of PWAs for access to experimental drugs. One doesn't demand compassion; one requests or pleads for it. And compassion is not, in our system of moral and legal figuring, something that anybody is compelled or obligated to give. In pointing this out, I stress that I am not denigrating kindness as a human motive generally, nor its specific role in prompting the release of drugs to the catastrophically ill. Real strides have been made in the last couple of years under compassion's banner. But it is important to see that the politics of compassion have limited the therapeutic options of PWAs, and it is even more important to see that they are wrong.

Rights are different. Once we know them, neither Americans nor Canadians beg for our rights – we demand them. And the appropriate response of our governments to the expression of a legitimate individual right isn't compassion – it is honour reflected in action. The logic of rights is much crisper and cleaner than the logic of compassion, and when they are a relevant feature of a conflict between individuals and the state, everybody's sense of what is due them, or required of them, becomes more clear. The situation then calls for adjudication, as opposed to either pleading or the endless varieties of pressure politics. Viewed in this light, the introduction of catastrophic rights may be seen to promise a revolution in the governance of experimental drugs.

It will not be, however, the sort of revolution which sweeps all restrictions aside. For although "rights talk" introduces a badly needed logical structure to the access issue, it doesn't lend itself – in the context of AIDS at least – to the provision of simple solutions. The problem is complex, and the solutions likewise, because the communicable nature of HIV infection guarantees that the public health crisis posed by it is everybody's business.

This can be seen clearly if we were to imagine, for a moment, that we possessed both a completely effective and safe vaccine against HIV, and an absolutely safe and effective treatment for those already infected with HIV, but who have not yet developed AIDS. If these two hoped-for discoveries were in place, AIDS would – from a practical standpoint – no longer be a communicable disease, and the public health threat posed by it would be immeasurably reduced. It would still represent an incalculable disaster, because countless thousands of human beings, whose immune systems had been destroyed earlier, would remain catastrophically ill. But since their personal catastrophe could no longer become anyone else's personal catastrophe, their illness would be, if I may speak so cold-bloodedly and objectively, their business – at least so far as any possible conflict with a vital public interest is concerned. My point here is that if AIDS were to come to an end with the lives of those who presently have it, the catastrophic rights of PWAs would be, for all practical purposes, absolute.

The real world confronts us, at least presently, with a much more difficult set of considerations. AIDS is not going to come to an end when those who have it now are gone. We know that without effective treatment for HIV infection, wave upon wave of disease is certain to break upon us from the ranks of those in whom the illness is incubating. Similarly, without an effective vaccine, we know that even the most cunning preventative programs cannot halt a sexually transmissible disease, but only slow it. AIDS presently represents a global threat of staggering proportions. We have, in the international as well as the national sense of "public," a vital public health interest in stopping it. By extension of this logic, we have a vital public interest in protecting, and if possible enhancing, the power of the single most important weapon we bring to the battle – our ability to make scientific medical progress.

So, on the one hand we have the special right of the catastrophically ill to exercise a greater than ordinary measure of control (that is, greater than the therapeutic authorities permit to those suffering from non-catastrophic illness) over their fight for their own lives, while on the other hand, we have the vital public interest of society in pressing the scientific search for the answer to the cruel riddle that has been posed us by this Sphinx of AIDS. To put it starkly: it would be nice to let everybody take whatever they wanted whenever they wanted it, but if we did, it might become practically impossible to figure out what works. And if we can't discover which medicines work, and which ones don't, we will remain powerless in the face of an epidemic which has ample power to decimate not just North American society, but *human* society.

As I pointed out earlier, one of science's most important tricks for getting answers from nature is to ask it the simplest possible questions in experimental settings that permit close attention to even a whispered answer. The relevant feature of this fact of scientific life, for catastrophic rights, is that a question such as "does DDI work?" almost certainly isn't simple enough to provide a useful basis for scientific work. Such a question sounds simple – just three little words – but really represents a cluster of longer – but actually simpler – questions, such as: given 500 asymptomatic persons at stage Gamma of HIV infection, how much better than the standard therapy (which presently is to do nothing) would it be for them to take dose X of DDI for six months? Or, given 500 AIDS people who are stable on AZT, how much better than their AZT therapy would it be for them to take dose X of DDI for six months? And so on.

Science needs to ask these long-winded questions because it has to expect that it almost certainly isn't working with an experimental "magic bullet." Only once or twice in an epoch will it be the happy lot of medical investigators to ask nature a question that gets a simple answer, such as: does penicillin work? That answer approached, in volume and drama, God's speech to Job from out of the whirlwind. But the answer to the question concerning us here – does DDI work? – will almost certainly be a qualified one. Recognizing that, medical scientists must design experiments which ask questions in a way that makes it possible for nature to give even a highly qualified answer. Otherwise, we can go from bad – which is getting no answer – to worse – which is getting a positively misleading one. Besides, even a highly qualified "yes" is a good answer. It introduces solid as opposed to nebulous hope, and may prove to be an opening that can be further widened through the focusing of scientific attention upon its established significance.

As per our earlier discussion of experimental controls, this is where the randomized control group fits into experimental work with human subjects. If there is a premium on being able to detect qualified or subtle answers from nature, we must design experiments which provide a carefully controlled background against which investigators can take the measure of such weak, but still significant, responses. However, control of the experiment can very well translate into control of the subjects. We must develop a framework within which to discharge our twin responsibilities of providing justice to individuals while attending to those needs of science which are inseparable from the protection of vital public health interests. Doing the right thing in this setting means attending to the special situation that obtains when an individual right conflicts with a vital public interest.

As was discussed in the section "Science and Rights," the general rule governing such a conflict is that the state should first seek to avoid restricting the right, but if restrictions are unavoidable, they should only go so far as is necessitated by the vital character of the overriding public interest. Therefore, the first possibility to be explored must be that of serving both masters. Can we design experimental trials of drugs which go forward under conditions of complete voluntarism? Can medical science adjust its agenda, as distinct from abandoning it, so that catastrophic subjects enter a trial *not* because the chance of being randomized into its experimental arm represents their only hope of receiving the drug they want to try, but because they believe that committing to the experiment makes sense for them? This is, as I have pointed out earlier, an empirical question. We must seek an answer to it with as much care as we insist upon bringing to the task of getting scientific answers to our questions about specific experimental drugs.

In this connection, there is already a cloud of controversy growing around the newly approved access channels which are presently "competing" with the various ongoing Phase II trials of DDI, Bristol-Meyers' new anti-viral, in the United States. In a November 9 1989 story in the *Los Angeles Times*, Marlene Cimons reported that fewer than 100 patients had enrolled in the studies, while about 1000 had elected to simply go on DDI in the newly approved, less formal clinical trials, which are collectively termed the parallel track. The piece is headlined "Lack of Volunteers May Hurt AIDS Drug Trials," and officials responsible for the formal trials are described as monitoring the situation closely, so as to tell whether the special Investigational New Drug provisions and the proposed parallel track are adversely impacting the research.

But can this particular test of the "two masters" option tell them anything that can be applied outside of its specific context? A quotation from the *Times* article suggests that it probably cannot:

> Federal health officials have insisted all along that individuals who were otherwise eligible for formal trials would not be allowed access to the drug through other channels. However, at the NIH meeting this week, some researchers suggested that the entry criteria for the formal studies may be too strict, enabling patients to use the easier alternative to get the drug, sources said.
>
> "People are asking for more flexibility," one researcher said.

"It's too easy to rule someone out and lose him to parallel track. We may have to loosen up the rules a little to attract the patients."

For example, one of the formal studies is designed to determine whether individuals who develop anemia taking AZT do better with DDI. To be eligible for the formal study, an individual must demonstrate that AZT has reduced the oxygen-carrying capacity of his blood by more than 40%, as measured through his level of hemoglobin.

"Many physicians would stop AZT before a patient's hemoglobin got that low, or give him a blood transfusion, so he would not qualify for the formal trial," one researcher said. "Also, if the physician has the option of getting his patient on DDI in a Treatment IND – which is easier than getting him into a formal trial – that's what he's going to do."

Thus, he said, in these circumstances, an individual might "never even know" that he qualified for a formal trial and would not be motivated to find out since the drug was available elsewhere.

Human experimentation which is designed around a need for subjects whose clinical condition could – in most circumstances – only be created by malpracticing physicians is, hopefully, not going to attract many recruits in the United States. It is not clear at the time of this writing whether the parallel tracks will have a serious impact on the formal trials of DDI. But it appears likely that they will. If so, it would be foolish to conclude on the basis of such evidence that genuinely voluntary trials of catastrophic therapies are impossible. In fact, it would be downright hypocritical to offer, in the name of the protection of real science, such a hopelessly unscientific test of the two masters thesis.

Ordinarily, catastrophic patients have never been especially sophisticated consumers or critics of medical treatment. They are, as a group, generally too sick for all of that. AIDS patients have been strikingly different in that their medical situation has typically permitted them sufficient time to develop a very high level of personal knowledge about their disease and its prospective treatments. Perhaps even more important than these personal opportunities, PWAs have created their own political and paramedical institutions to accelerate individual efforts to take control of their situation. What this means back at the clinic is that the willingness or unwillingness of PWAs to be voluntary subjects in an experiment can be fairly accurately determined by scientists simply asking themselves: "Would *I* enroll as a subject in this particular experiment if I were a PWA *and* I could gain access to the experimental drug – presuming that I wanted to try it – in some other way?" Very many investigators answer, honestly, that they wouldn't submit to the conditions of randomization and blindness if they were catastrophically ill. Not, at least, in the context of the experimental designs that have typified work on HIV.

What is to be done? Yogi Berra once said that if the fans won't come to the game, there's nothing you can do to stop them. And if catastrophically ill human subjects won't enlist in poorly designed trials, there will be less and less to be gained in trying to force their participation. The good old days (or the bad old days – depending upon your perspective) of routine coercion are, for several reasons, over. The system of experimental trials has to be "brought to the patients" by way of a revolutionary change. This means that the initiation of formal trials must be more speedily and flexibly responsive to the emergence of promising leads, and the trials themselves must be imaginatively designed so as to run more quickly and effectively with fewer subjects. Both conceptual and material fat has to be ruthlessly pared from the process, so that it makes more sense for medically sophisticated subjects to become genuine volunteers. Just about everybody who counts agrees that this could at least possibly be done; that is, everybody agrees that there is substantial running room for science in the direction of leaner, smarter trials of catastrophic therapies. In fact, the liberalizing reforms of the last couple of years have, beyond their immediate accomplishments, served to provide at least a glimpse of what remains to be accomplished. More progress will depend directly upon the creation of the political will for it, and the related determination on the part of governments to take a greater measure of financial responsibility for the ability of their therapeutic authorities to protect the conditions for scientific progress without unjust restriction of the therapeutic autonomy of catastrophic patients.

How can this be done? Some of the most promising leads have emerged from the community, as PWAs and their physicians in the U.S. have not only organized and conducted their own trials of promising treatments, but have done so in ways which meet all FDA and other legal requirements. These community-based research initiatives have moved from modest beginnings in early 1988 to a position of established, and growing, contribution. When the FDA finally approved aerosol pentamidine in July 1989, it was on the basis of data from studies begun by two of the pioneers in community-based research – the County Community Consortium in San Francisco, and the Community Research Initiative in New York. And the cooperation of the pharmaceutical company Genelabs with community based groups in Project Inform allowed the speedy determination of the dangers of its Compound Q, which were published as preliminary findings in an October 1989 press conference in Washington. These achievements were made possible not by disregarding the rights of patients, but by approaching the scientific task from the perspective of the medically sophisticated PWA and his physician ally. Primary treatment physicians and PWAs were active in the formulation of the trial protocols, rather than mere passive consumers of them. Significantly, in his discussion of community-based research in the August 11 1989 *AIDS Treatment News*, John S. James reports that emergency funding for the pentamidine study had to be provided by the drug's licensee, LyphoMed Inc., after the U.S. National Institutes of Health had unexpectedly refused to fund it. In general, community-based research organizations are without sufficient established or institutionalized sources of operating funds.

But what about the toughest cases? What happens after we have done all that we can reasonably do – or at least have done the obvious things that are already done by community-based research groups – to conduct a well-designed trial of a promising drug under conditions of complete voluntarism, and we fail to attract sufficient subjects? What happens when both masters cannot be served? Setting aside, for the sake of the question, a range of relevant considerations (such as the vital character of the particular trial) as settled, my conviction is that in such an instance the vital public interest legitimately prevails, and overrides the competing catastrophic rights. But then, of course, the overridden rights do not subside into nothingness, but continue to exert a special and continuing form of pressure on the situation. The overriding of an individual right for the sake of a vital public interest must automatically raise a particular question about proportionality: how can the vital component of this public interest be served with the least possible limitation of the individual rights conflicting with it?

There are several plausible answers to this question in the case of AIDS research. Forced to turn to some version of the devil that we know, it may make sense to try an experimental design which "captures" subjects, in the manner of the current Phase II DDI trials. As was noted in the *L.A. Times* article quoted above, the central idea of the informal parallel track was that it could *not* compete with the trials. This was to be guaranteed by denying entry to the informal studies to patients who qualified for any of the formal trials. Thus, if you fulfilled the inclusion criteria of one of the controlled experiments, and wanted to try DDI, the only way you could possibly get it was to volunteer for one of the trials and take your chances with the randomization. In fact, then, these trials are not perfectly voluntary. They really represent a kind of compromise between the old trial system and the demands of PWA advocates. As such, and with better-designed experiments, they might well represent a reasonable option to be explored by a society seeking a proportional solution – *after* an earnest effort to make a truly voluntary system of trials had failed. Vital to the success of such proportional option would be the inclusion of community-based research groups. To the extent that individual rights are ever sacrificed for medical progress against AIDS, their sacrifice will yield benefits in direct proportion to the participation of the affected groups in the key decisions about experimental trials.

Democracy can seem a tiresome waste of time and money. It was Oscar Wilde, I believe, who complained that the trouble with it was that it took too many evenings. The point to be taken by democratic governments in this connection is that self-government is at the centre of what we are and what we do. Because of this, I think it is important that the American and Canadian governments create appropriate tribunals for the adjudication of claims of catastrophic rights, and include PWA organizations in their composition. Initiating such an institutionalization of catastrophic rights will make our efforts to defeat AIDS more effective and hence, in the medium to long term, maybe cheaper as well. As things stand now, AIDS research is threatened almost in direct proportion to the extent that it is undertaken without sensitive regard for the rights of PWAs. Like it or not, this has become a political fact of research life in the eighties, and there is no prospect that it will disappear in the nineties. One can see it as an instance of the emergence of a pressure group which must be mollified, tricked, or crushed, or one can see it as an instance of the emergence of a group with a claim about a particular form of patient's right. The latter option has, to my mind, the twin advantages of conforming to the truth, and suggesting an established framework – the provision of justice and fairness – within which this issue can be located and worked through.

From the perspective of the state, "worked through" may be freely translated as "effectively governed." Government doesn't need to apologize for governing when it is confronted with a deadly, infectious, and incurable disease. The social control of medicines is, simply, a legitimate mission of our therapeutic authorities as they work for the full range of public health interests associated with AIDS. The issue is not whether to govern catastrophic drugs, but how.

Catastrophic rights do not pose a fresh obstacle in the path of North American regulatory authorities as they seek our social benefit. To be sure, and especially to the extent that they embody considerations of justice, these rights are *for* Persons With AIDS, but they are also *for* society and its therapeutic authorities. The logic of rights makes possible the genuine adjudication of conflict between individual and public claims, and this is, in our present circumstance, a painfully missing and sorely missed capability of our regulatory systems.

Catastrophic rights are, as I admitted at the outset, an innovation. But just as the AIDS epidemic has created an urgent need for carefully considered scientific innovation, it has revealed a parallel need for sensible and sensitive innovation in governance as well. Seen in this light, the institutionalization of catastrophic rights will not disarm our therapeutic authorities, but will rather provide them with a timely and potent reinforcement of their resources.

In closing, I want to return to a comment made to me a couple of years ago by Kevin Brown, shortly after the Vancouver Persons With Aids Society (of which he was the spokesperson) complained to the B.C. Civil Liberties Association about access to experimental drugs. I was in the process of writing the original brief prepared by the BCCLA on the issue, and having a working lunch with Kevin downtown. He had arrived, he told me, at the point at which he recognized, clearly and unequivocally, that he would not live to see the fruition of this project, or of very many others that he was responsible for. About this he said that he had come to realize that there was very much more to the world than him, that he was only a tiny part of the human community, that he was even really only a very small part of his immediate community of gay men and PWAs. Small to start with, and about to disappear. I was braced for what William James once called the "bass note" of existence, but that wasn't where my lunch companion was going. He said, rather, that realizing all of this was among the greatest joys he had found in his life, because it had revealed to him how lucky he had been to wake up in time to recognize what a community was, and to learn at least a little of what it meant to really take up one's work in it. By spreading out from himself in his efforts for PWAs, by devoting himself to such work, he had become – in the deepest sense of the phrase – "well-connected." "I leave the best of myself behind in the work," he said simply, "in lively partnership with those who continue it."

He was one of those whom death had sophisticated. AIDS and those who have it are, in their turn, seeking to transform – to make more sophisticated, if you will – our conception of the morality of experimentation on the catastrophically ill. My contention is that they have a genuine lesson to teach, and that their case for moving from the politics of compassion to the politics of rights has both merit and applicable force in our present situation. What now remains to be seen is if our therapeutic authorities are as educable – as docile in the face of an opportunity for learning – as was Kevin Brown at his end.

Printed in Canada